THE RAINCOAST
KITCHEN

THE RAINCOAST KITCHEN

COASTAL CUISINE WITH A DASH OF HISTORY

The Museum at Campbell River

COOKBOOK COMMITTEE

Sue Cowan • Gerrie Dinsley • Janice Kenyon
Jackie MacNaughton • Irene Ross • Thelma Silkens
Jay Stewart • Jeanette Taylor • Joan Whitmore

HARBOUR PUBLISHING

HARBOUR PUBLISHING
P.O. Box 219
Madeira Park, BC Canada V0N 2H0
Cover, page design and composition by Roger Handling, Terra Firma Design
Cover illustration by Kim LaFave
Printed and bound in Canada

Photograph credits:
BCARS—British Columbia Archives & Records Service;
CRM—Campbell River Museum;
UBC—Special Collections, University of British Columbia Library;
VMM—Vancouver Maritime Museum; VPL—Vancouver Public Library.

Canadian Cataloguing in Publication Data
Main entry under title:
The raincoast kitchen

ISBN 1-55017-144-5

1. Cookery, Canadian—British Columbia style. 2. Cookery—
Pacific Coast (B.C.) 3. British Columbia—History—
Miscellanea. I. Campbell River Museum & Archives.
TX715.6R35 1996   641.59711'1   C96-910087-6

Dedicated to
the memory of
Estelle Elizabeth Inman
whose enthusiasm for the museum cookbook
inspired its realization.

Caesar Kay-Nichols was one of the grand old characters who pioneered the Sayward Valley. Trapper, timber cruiser and bon vivant, he was a keen photographer and took this picture himself. Photo courtesy of Frances Duncan.

Didn't somebody famous once say you couldn't really claim to know a people until you sat down and broke bread with them? If they didn't, they should have, because there's more than a crumb of truth in the idea. When you taste your first mouthful of sun-dried sockeye salmon soaked in eulachon grease, you suddenly know something about the way the First Nations people of the Northwest Coast lived that no amount of musty texts or well-wrought totem poles can tell you.

This book opens a floodgate of flavours from the people of the raincoast— the people who have carved out their living between the evergreen jungles and the craggy coastline that stretches along the shores of Washington, British Columbia and Alaska. To sample the dishes this book contains—from salmon barbecued in the traditional First Nations style, to hearty cookhouse fare from the old-time logging camps, to fashionable contemporary cuisine given a special saltchuck savour by resourceful raincoast chefs—is to taste the essence of this uniquely convoluted place where in one day you can visit tiny fishing communities, remote light stations, centuries-old Native villages and dynamic young cities.

This book is a result of two powerful enthusiasms: for great grub and for the fascinating history of the Pacific Northwest. How it came about is a kind of miracle in itself.

Among the vigorous communities of the Inside Passage, Campbell River is perhaps the one that remains closest to its roots in the small coastal settlements of yesteryear. This is nowhere more evident than in its beautiful and very active museum, which is widely recognized as one of the finest in the coastal region. The staff and volunteers, whose enthusiasm for all things local coloured their approach to museum social events, developed a wonderful tradition of exploring the best in regional cooking styles. Members' nights, annual general meetings, fund-raisers and celebrations all became occasions for trying out mouth-watering appetizers, imaginative salads and irresistible desserts. Legends grew quickly and constant requests for the more popular recipes soon led to the proposal for a book that would preserve this most delectable of the museum's collections.

Once the Cookbook Project got underway, museum staff put its considerable research powers into high gear, combing the recipe files of local families for the treasured secrets of coastal cookery, all of which were carefully tested on friends, relatives and unsuspecting guest speakers. When the results were finally laid out, the staff's overriding passion for regional history asserted itself in the form of archival quotations, historic photographs and marginal notes on old-time cooking methods sometimes going back before the arrival of the white people.

The end result is the book you see before you—not only a book on cooking and not only a document on coastal history, but a perfectly delicious blend of both.

Break bread with us and taste the raincoast.

Howard White,
Publisher

Mrs. Nixon of Twin Islands,
BC, back from
a successful hunt in the
rainforest, c. 1912.
CRM 5444.

CONTENTS

*A leisurely breakfast in the garden is the best way
to start the day.
Henry and Agnes Twidle, Granite Bay, BC.
c. 1930*

CRM 6951

BREAD & BREAKFASTS

Donkey Boiler Coffee

"**A**round about eleven o'clock in the morning when you were all tired out, ready for your break, you began to think about your lunch and, even more than your lunch, you thought about your coffee. Loggers' coffee in those years wasn't made on a stove at all and wasn't put in a thermos. They made it in the firebox of the donkey engine. The firebox is where they would have a roaring fire to keep steam in the boiler, because everything ran by steam in those years.

The loggers would be waiting and waiting and waiting and then eleven-thirty finally came and the engineer would blow his whistle; he would go *woooo woo*—one long and one short—and that meant lunch time. So everybody would drop their gloves and head to the donkey engine.

As soon as that whistle blew, the fireman, whose job it was to stoke the fires, would start making the coffee. On the donkey engine deck he would have an old soup box or a big milk container. In it he'd store a big bag of coffee and a lot of half-pound tobacco tins for the loggers to drink their coffee from, we didn't have cups.

He would take a great big lard pail, one of the great big storage pails that holds two or three gallons of water, off a hook and he'd reach for what he called his injector hose. This is one of the hoses that had hot, hot steam from the donkey boiler. He'd put some spring water in his bucket first and he'd take the injector hose and whoosh,

Two loggers enjoying a break. A photograph from the album of logger Mel Parker, taken in Call Inlet, 1941. CRM 18981.

he'd send a big jet of hot steam into it and it would bring it right from cold to boiling in nothing flat.

Then the important thing, he'd take about two pounds of coffee, which is quite a lot of coffee, and

he'd dump it into this furiously boiling water. Then he'd take what they called the slice bar, one of the steel pokers that they used for poking up the fire in the firebox, and he'd hang his pail with his coffee makings on one end of the slice bar and he'd ram it right into the white-hot donkey boiler.

In a second it would be blowing steam all over the place, it boiled so quickly. He'd hold it there for a while and let it have a good bubble, good boil. The heat was terrible, his face would be all screwed up from the heat. Then he'd set the pail on the donkey deck and he'd grab another of these bags of cold water, drinking water, and he'd pour about two quarts into the coffee; that was to settle it down. And then the coffee was ready for drinking.

The fellows would all swarm on the donkey engine and grab their empty tobacco cans and they'd take a dip into the big steaming bucket of coffee and get a half-pound can of coffee, which is quite a lot. And there'd be canned milk, 'canned cow' we called it, and sugar in bags and we'd fix our coffee the way we wanted it. I liked mine quite sweet without very much milk in it. Then we'd all sit with our lunches—we brought our lunches from camp if we were working out on a job.

Bill Crabe, resting during lunch break near Port Neville, 1939. Dick Hopkins is on the stump. CRM 5518.

A group of men around a steam donkey from P.B. Anderson's outfit, part of the Knox Bay Logging crew. CRM 5156

we'd have maybe a refill of coffee and some fellows would even have two refills of coffee.

It was good coffee. A man with big feet could walk on it. It was the best coffee I ever tasted in my life, even if you did have to fish bits of burnt twig and charcoal out of it every now and then. But it had a taste, I think maybe from the quick, really savage boil in the white hot steam, that no other coffee anywhere else ever got, so we loved it.

I'd give a lot for a can of it right now."

Arthur "Bill" Mayse

Bill Mayse told this story to Jeanette Taylor and her children shortly before his death. His wife, Win, died only two weeks later. Win's knowledge of local history and her engaging manner entranced countless visitors to the museum on Saturday afternoons. Bill's mastery as storyteller and his devotion to detail, together with his characteristic writing style, were evident in the label copy he wrote for the logging exhibits in the old museum. Bill and Win Mayse were incomparable friends of the museum for more than twenty years. We miss them.

We called them 'nose bags' because they were a brown paper bag with, oh, about four sandwiches in it, four big heavy sandwiches made of some meat or other, whatever was going in camp. And there'd be a great big piece of pie, about a quarter of an apple pie. That would be your dessert and a couple of jam sandwiches and some cookies. That made a pretty hefty lunch but we were hungry.

We'd been working hard all morning so we were ready to eat. We'd open our lunch bags and start in on our sandwiches and then we'd reach for our coffee. Nothing tasted as good as that first drink of what we called 'donkey boiler coffee' after a hard morning's work.

While we were eating, the big ravens that come around every logging operation in the woods, would come looking for food and we'd throw them scraps of our sandwiches. Everyone was quite relaxed and happy. And

At Cape Scott, on the northern-most tip of Vancouver Island, people transported heavy loads over settlers' trails by strapping packboards to their backs—a practice that gave rise to legends like this one.

"A brother and sister—both very strong—left the store, each carrying a pack. When they arrived at their cabin several miles up the trail, the brother chided the sister for having forgotten a sack of flour. The sister, conscious of her triumph, threw open the door of a stove still strapped to her packboard, to reveal the added fifty pound burden."

Cape Scott Gazette,
November 13, 1985

Rhubarb Pecan Muffins

Makes 12

1	**egg, beaten**	1
¼ cup	**oil**	50 mL
¾ cup	**orange juice**	175 mL
2 tsp	**grated orange rind**	10 mL
¾ cup	**chopped pecans**	175 mL

Preheat oven to 350°F (180°C). Mix egg, oil, orange juice, rind and pecans together.

2 cups	**flour**	500 mL
¾ cup	**sugar**	175 mL
1 ½ tsp	**baking powder**	7 mL
½ tsp	**soda**	2 mL
1 tsp	**salt**	5 mL

In a separate bowl, combine all dry ingredients. Mix with wet ingredients just until all flour is moistened.

1¼ cups	**finely chopped rhubarb**	300 mL

Fold in rhubarb. Pour into greased muffin tins and bake for 30 minutes.

Irene Ross

Crew members from International Timber and their families enjoy a July 1st picnic at "Big Cedars," near Forbes Landing, 1921. CRM 14942.

Cornmeal Bread

Makes 2 loaves

½ cup	**cornmeal**	125 mL
1 cup	**boiling water**	250 mL
1 tsp	**salt**	5 mL

Pour cornmeal into boiling salted water and cook, stirring vigorously, for about 4 minutes or until thick. Cool in a large mixing bowl.

2 pkgs	**active dry yeast**	2 pkgs
1 Tbsp	**sugar**	15 mL
½ cup	**warm water**	125 mL

Combine yeast, sugar and water and let it sit for 5 minutes or until foamy. Pour into mixing bowl with the cooled cornmeal. Mix well.

1 cup	**milk, warmed**	250 mL
1½ Tbsp	**salt**	23 mL
¼ cup	**dark brown sugar**	50 mL
4–4½ cups	**unbleached flour**	900–1025 mL

VPL 1432.

Add milk, salt and sugar. Add flour 1 cup (250 mL) at a time, stirring well after each addition. When well blended, turn out on floured board and knead until smooth and elastic, about 10 minutes, adding more flour as needed. Place dough in a large buttered bowl and turn to coat with butter on all sides. Cover and set in a warm place about 1½ hours or until doubled in size.

Punch down and turn out on a floured board. Cut in half, shape into 2 loaves and let rest. Place dough in 2 buttered loaf pans, cover and let rise again until doubled in bulk, about 1 hour.

Preheat oven to 425°F (220°C). Bake bread for 10 minutes, then lower the temperature to 350°F (180°C) and continue baking for 20–25 minutes until the bread is browned and sounds hollow when removed from pans.

Irene Ross

" A logger called Roughhouse Pete had the reputation that when he didn't like the food, in the morning he would put on his caulk boots and walk up and down the breakfast tables and kick all the food and dishes off. That was the end of his job, of course."
Mel Parker, *CRM aural history*
Born in 1920, Mel Parker started working in the woods at the age of twelve.

Focaccia / Bogoli

Makes one 8" (20 cm) focaccia/bogoli

1½ tsp	**active dry yeast**	7 mL
½ cup	**warm water**	125 mL

Sprinkle yeast over warm water and stir until dissolved.

1¼ cups	**flour**	300 mL
½ tsp	**salt**	2 mL

Combine flour and salt in a separate bowl.

3 Tbsp	**olive oil**	45 mL
¼ tsp	**salt**	1 mL

Whisk 2 Tbsp (30 mL) olive oil into dissolved yeast and stir this into the flour. Add more flour if necessary to make a soft dough that doesn't stick to your fingers and let rest for 20 minutes. Shape dough into a round about 8" (20 cm) in diameter and about 1" (2.5 cm) thick.

Preheat oven to 400°F (200°C). Place dough on greased cookie sheet, brush with remaining olive oil and sprinkle salt on top. Bake for 15 minutes.

Irene Ross

"There was a big breakfast—they always had just killed a cow so there was liver or bacon and porridge and fried potatoes. After breakfast Granny picked fresh vegetables in the garden and their dinner was at twelve o'clock. In the afternoon Granny rested and read then she changed out of her house dress for supper—cold meat from dinner and salads and canned fruit."

Irene McMann, speaking in 1992 about summer at her grandparents' home (Alfred and Anna Joyce) in the early years of the century.

Dorothy Spencer at "Homewood," the Walker farm in Gowlland Harbour, 1936. CRM 6727.

Fried Bread

Serves 6

6 cups	**flour**	1350 mL
1 tsp	**salt**	5 mL
6 tsp	**baking powder**	30 mL
	water	
	oil or lard	

Combine dry ingredients and add enough water to make mixture sticky. Dust fingers with flour and take about a rounded tablespoon of the dough. Pat the dough back and forth in hands, handling lightly. Do not knead as with yeast dough or bread will be tough. Flatten dough ball to about ½'' (1 cm) thick. Melt enough lard in frying pan so there is ¼'' (.5 cm) liquid in bottom of pan. Cook flattened patties until golden brown. Flip and cook the other side. Cooked bread may be placed in a roasting pan lined with a brown paper bag while other bread patties are being fried. Best eaten hot. Especially good dipped in syrup.

Amy Quatell (Muksun)

A portrait of Chief Billy Assu of Cape Mudge, taken by photo-historian Henry Twidle, c. 1915. CRM 9105.

A Henderson Breakfast

Serves 1–2

8 oz	**bacon, chopped**	225 g
	chopped onion to taste	
	shredded cabbage to taste	

Fry bacon until half cooked. Add onion and cabbage and stir-fry until done.

	leftover cooked rice (optional)	
3	**eggs, beaten**	3

Sprinkle leftover rice on top and add beaten eggs. Stir-fry again until hot throughout.

	seasonings to taste	

Season to taste and serve.

Sam Henderson

Dining Etiquette in the Old Days

"**A**s whenever they cook, they always calculate to have an abundance for all the guests, a profusion in this respect being considered as the highest luxury, much more is usually set before them than they can eat. That which is left in the king's tray he sends to his house for his family, by one of his slaves, as do the chiefs theirs, while those who eat from the same tray and who generally belong to the same family, take it home as common stock, or each one receives his portion, which is distributed on the spot. This custom appeared very singular to my companion and myself, and it was a most awkward thing for us at first, to have to lug home with us, in our hands or arms, the blubber or fish that we received at these times; but we soon became reconciled to it, and were very glad of an opportunity to do it."

Narrative of the Adventures of John R. Jewitt, 1815

17

Peasant Date Bread

Makes 2 loaves

1¼ cups	**warm water**	300 mL
1 Tbsp	**molasses**	15 mL
1 Tbsp	**yeast**	15 mL

Combine water and molasses well and sprinkle the yeast over. Let it brew.

½ cup	**sunflower seeds**	125 mL
½ cup	**flax seeds**	125 mL
⅔ cup	**warm water**	150 mL
¼ cup	**instant milk powder**	50 mL
1 Tbsp	**oil**	15 mL
1½ tsp	**salt**	7 mL
1 Tbsp	**lemon juice**	15 mL

Combine next 7 ingredients, mixing well. Add yeast mixture and stir again.

2 cups	**whole wheat flour**	500 mL
¼ cup	**raisins or chopped dates**	50 mL

Add 2 cups (500 mL) flour and raisins and blend with electric mixer for about 5 minutes. (You can also use a bread hook or a food processor.)

3–4 cups	**whole wheat flour**	700–900 mL

Add another 3–4 cups (700–900 mL) flour and mix well, turn out and knead. Cover and let rise in warm place. Punch down, shape into two loaves. Let rise until double.

	sesame seeds (optional)	

Preheat oven to 350°F (180°C).
Sprinkle loaves with sesame seeds and bake for 40–50 minutes.

Leona Taylor

I start this bread during my lunch hour (12:00), let it double in my sun-warmed car, punch down and reset during coffee break (2:30), then drive home at 4:00 and bake the loaves.

Leona Taylor

Potato Bread

Makes 1 loaf

1 cup	**mashed potatoes**	250 mL

Use leftover mashed potatoes, or boil fresh potatoes in their skins until tender, peel and mash while still warm. Cool.

1 pkg	**active dry yeast**	1 pkg
½ cup	**warm water**	125 mL
3 Tbsp	**flour**	45 mL

Dissolve yeast in warm water. Then mix well with flour in large bowl. This is your starter. Let this rise for 30 minutes.

2 cups	**warm water**	500 mL
1½ Tbsp	**salt**	23 mL
8 cups	**flour**	1800 mL

Add warm water and salt, then flour and mashed potatoes. Mix well. Knead dough until supple, about 14 minutes, and shape into a ball. Put dough into an oiled bowl and turn to coat ball. Place in a warm, draft-free spot for 1–2 hours, until double in bulk. Remove dough, punch down and knead for 5 minutes.

½ Tbsp	**caraway seeds** (optional)	8 mL

Shape into a large round loaf, sprinkle with caraway seeds if desired, and place in buttered 12" (30 cm) skillet. Let rise again for 30–35 minutes.

Preheat oven to 400°F (200°C). Brush loaf with water and make a slight cut across the top. Bake for 1 hour or until browned. Bread is done when it sounds hollow when tapped.

Irene Ross

Sunnyside Farm, Quadra Island, BC.
The Yeatman family and their
hop-covered house, 1903.
CRM 4255.

"Yeast that will keep for weeks—Pour a pint of boiling water over a dessert spoonful of hops, boil in a little water and let it steep for a while, pour this on one good sized grated potato and stir. Put both back into the saucepan with two tablespoons of sugar, one dessert spoon of salt, a good tablespoon flour, wet with a little water, then add to the ingredients and let all boil up."

from The King's Daughter Cookery Book, *compiled by Mrs. R. B. McMicking of Victoria BC, c. 1904. Recipe contributed by* **Mrs. F. Page.**

"Hazenfratz' Hop Beer—Boil five quarts water and six ounces hops for three hours then strain the liquor. Add to it five quarts water, four ounces bruised ginger root, boil again 20 minutes. Strain and add four pounds sugar. When lukewarm put in yeast. In 24 hours it will be ready for bottling."

found in an old house in Victoria, once the home of the Hazenfratz family, who owned breweries in Victoria and Nanaimo at the turn of the century.

Cheese & Bread Soufflé

Serves 6

8–10	**slices bread, buttered**	8–10
1 lb	**cheddar cheese, sliced**	450 g
4	**green onions, minced**	4

In a buttered baking dish, alternate layers of bread, cheese and green onion.

5	**eggs, beaten lightly**	5
1 Tbsp	**prepared mustard**	15 mL
3 cups	**milk**	700 mL
¼ tsp	**cayenne pepper**	1 mL
	salt to taste	

Whisk eggs with mustard, milk, cayenne and salt. Pour slowly over bread and cheese. Let stand 30 minutes.

¼ cup	**bread crumbs**	50 mL
¼ cup	**grated parmesan cheese**	50 mL
2 Tbsp	**butter**	30 mL

Preheat oven to 350°F (180°C).
Mix crumbs and parmesan and sprinkle evenly over top. Dot with butter.
Bake 50–60 minutes at 350°F (180°C). This will puff up like a soufflé and should be served at once.

Thelma Silkens

"Logging camp cooks always were temperamental. If they weren't crazy when they started cooking, they were generally crazy before they finished. A good many were alcoholics. They were very good cooks. There were very few Chinese cooks or women cooks in the early days. You'd never see women cooks for the really big crews.

A lot of the cooks that travelled around in those days were black-balled from some camps. They were some of the best cooks but they weren't dependable from the drinking point of view."

Mel Parker, *CRM aural history*

Gourmet Ham & Honey Mustard Buns

Makes 16 buns

1 pkg	**active dry yeast**	1 pkg
1 Tbsp	**sugar**	15 mL
¾ cup	**warm water**	175 mL

Combine yeast, sugar and water and let it sit for 5 minutes or until foamy.

2 Tbsp	**butter**	30 mL
½ cup	**milk**	125 mL

Melt butter, add milk and heat to lukewarm. Add to yeast mixture.

3½ cups	**flour**	825 mL
2 tsp	**salt**	10 mL
1 tsp	**chopped fresh basil or savory**	5 mL

Add flour, salt and herbs. Stir until it forms a ball. Knead on floured surface. Add as much as ¼ cup (50 mL) more flour to prevent sticking. Knead for 10 minutes until smooth and elastic. Place dough in buttered bowl and turn to coat all sides. Let rise, covered, in a warm place for 1 hour or until double in bulk. Turn dough onto floured surface and roll into a 21x14" (53x35 cm) rectangle.

¼ cup	**Dijon mustard**	50 mL
1 Tbsp	**honey**	15 mL
⅔ lb	**Muenster cheese, grated**	300 g
12 oz	**black forest ham, sliced**	340 g
	chutney and additional Dijon mustard to taste	

Combine mustard and honey and spread over dough. Sprinkle with Muenster cheese. Cover cheese with ham and, starting with a long side, roll up jelly-roll fashion. Cut roll crosswise into 16 equal pieces and transfer to buttered muffin tins. Let rise again, covered, in warm place for 45 minutes until almost double in bulk.

Preheat oven to 375°F (190°C). Bake for 30 minutes until golden. Serve warm with chutney and additional mustard.

The bread may be made a day in advance. Keep it wrapped and chilled.

Jeanette Taylor

Buckwheat Pancakes
Ol' Leather's Sunday Morning Special

Serves 6

¾ cup	**rice flour**	175 mL
¾ cup	**buckwheat flour**	175 mL
pinch	**salt**	pinch
½ tsp	**baking powder**	2 mL

Mix all dry ingredients together.

3	**egg yolks**	3
½ tsp	**vanilla**	2 mL
1½ cups	**milk**	375 mL

Mix egg yolks, vanilla and milk in a separate bowl. Make a depression in the dry ingredients, pour in milk mixture and mix well.

3	**egg whites, stiffly beaten**	3

Gently fold beaten egg whites into batter. Fry on preheated hot griddle.

honey, maple syrup, yoghurt, applesauce, sliced bananas

Spread honey or maple syrup over the pancakes and put several tablespoons of yoghurt on top. Smother the yoghurt in applesauce and sliced bananas. Or serve the pancakes with any combination of your favourite toppings.

Gerry Coté

"We would reach the camp and open the cook-house door, and feel how good it was to take our seats alongside the boys at breakfast. The lamps would be lighted, for it would be still dark indoors at half-past six, the cook-house would look bright and cosy—stove-wood stacked all round the walls breast-high; slabs of bacon hanging from the roof above; canned stuff—peas, beans, tomatoes, fruit, syrup, beef, and mutton bright and shining, neatly piled on shelves; sacks of onions, potatoes, rice, beans and flour at the far end where Pong Sam in spotless white would be busy at his stove flapping hot-cakes with swift, sure movements, bringing plates piled with them to table, answering calls for tea and coffee. Someone probably would have been out a few days before and shot a buck. The fried meat would smell good and look good upon the long table among the plates of fried ham, beans and bacon, potatoes, butter, syrup, cream and milk, and good yeast bread..."

M. A. Grainger, Woodsmen of the West, *writing about breakfast in a logging camp at Knight Inlet (Coula Inlet)*

Photo: UBC

Dining Out at Minstrel Island

Once in the late 1940s when I was in the bush flying business the deputy minister of transport came out from Ottawa to survey his western domain and I was honoured with the task of showing him around the upper coast. We flew him to Minstrel Island, because it was a typical logging community, and we arrived just in time for lunch.

At this time there was only one place to eat in Minstrel—Red's Sea Diner, operated by an ex-camp cook named Red Mahon. The diner sat on a small floating scow and consisted of a back half where Red and his missus slept, and a business half where Red worked his magic. This contained an oil-burning range, a sink and a work table. Pots, pans, ladles, cleavers hung from spikes pounded into the ceiling. The customers' area boasted a plank counter eight feet long, with four stools. Each stool was of the same design—an upright two-by-four, three feet high, with a one-foot two-by-

four spiked crossways on top to sit on. It looked like Red was expecting parrots instead of people.

To get to the diner you had to walk along a floating log with no handrail. The clientele Red catered to didn't need handrails.

The deputy minister of transport did need one, and it was only with much reeling and whooping we got him aboard and positioned him gingerly on one of the parrot perches. Red's menu was one of those that offered breakfast all day long. In fact it didn't offer anything else. He spread his hands on the counter and bellowed, "All right, you bastards, whaddya want? Ya can have enny-

thing as long as it's bacon and eggs. Ya wannem over or straight up? Cuz you're gonna get 'em straight up!"

With that he wheeled around to his stove, grabbed a handful of eggs, splashed them into a sizzling black frying pan by crunching them in his fists two at a time, slapped a bunch of bacon onto a smoking griddle, slid everything onto plates, stripped the fat off the griddle, flapped down half a dozen slices of white bread, flipped them once and presto! Bacon and eggs and toast a la Red.

Years later the deputy minister was still talking about it.

Jim Spilsbury, Spilsbury's Coast

Minstrel Island, home of Red's Floating Sea Diner. W.E. Nicholson photo.

Clam Fritters

Serves 6

1½ cups	**flour**	375 mL
½ tsp	**salt**	2 mL
2 tsp	**baking powder**	10 mL
1 tsp	**baking soda**	5 mL
	water	

Combine dry ingredients. Add enough water to make a stiff batter.

4 cups	**minced clams**	900 mL
1 cup	**chopped celery**	250 mL
1 cup	**chopped onion**	250 mL

Add clams, then vegetables. Mix well.

	oil for frying

Heat oil in frying pan. Drop in a spoonful of batter, cook until golden brown, then turn and cook the other side. Leftover batter may be kept in the refrigerator for a few days to make fresh fritters as desired.

Bill Henderson

"Our family used to dig clams at Gowlland Harbour [Quadra Island]. All the boys piled onto my Dad's little gas boat, his cod boat. One time we had gone over to Gowlland for a late tide, about ten o'clock at night. Since I was so young, I think I was eight, it was my job to gather the clams as my Dad dug. I stuck my hand in where he was digging and stuck my finger right in a clam. I was crying and screaming and it wouldn't come off. The only way my Dad could get it off was to smash the clam against a rock to break it up."

Bill Henderson,
Henderson, a Kwakw̱ak̲a'wakw artist, son of Sam and May Henderson, grew up in Campbell River in the 1950s and '60s.

Beach scene, Queen Charlotte Islands. The islands are famous for their rich razor clam beds. BCARS 34279.

Good company, plenty of food and a Quadra Picnic.
1912
CRM 12825

APPETIZERS

Roderick Haig-Brown and his children at their home in Campbell River, c. 1950. CRM 2476.

"This was fabulous country— that was what attracted me to it. It was tremendously exciting to an eighteen-year-old from a world of fishing and hunting. Campbell River was the logical choice—the nearest place with a road to the outside, a hospital and a school; pretty stable. It was the first place I had seen on Vancouver Island that had houses with hot and cold running water. I wanted a bit of civilization. There were about five hundred people here. Most were stump ranchers of one sort or another."

Roderick Haig-Brown,
CRM aural history. Haig-Brown was a renowned writer, magistrate, angling enthusiast and passionate conservationist who lived beside the Campbell River for many years. He was the author of twenty-five books, including several classics on fly fishing.

Crab Meat Canapé

Makes 6 cups (1.5 L)
Chill 4 hours

1 cup	**cream cheese**	250 g
10 oz	**condensed mushroom soup**	284 mL
1 tsp	**curry powder**	5 mL

Melt cream cheese. Blend in mushroom soup and curry. Heat to very hot.

1 pkg	**gelatin**	1 pkg
¼ cup	**water**	50 mL

Dissolve gelatin in water.

1 cup	**chopped onion**	250 mL
1 cup	**chopped celery**	250 mL
1 cup	**crab meat, fresh cooked or canned**	250 mL
1 cup	**mayonnaise**	250 mL

Add gelatin and remaining ingredients to cheese mixture and mix well. Put into a 6-cup (1.5 L) mold and refrigerate for at least 4 hours.
Slice and serve on crackers.

Judy Price Sturgis

Crab Pastriettes

Makes 18

Filling:

½ cup	**chopped fresh parsley**	125 mL
¼ tsp	**onion salt**	1 mL
8 oz	**canned crab meat, drained**	225 g
1½ cups	**grated cheddar cheese**	375 mL
2	**eggs, well beaten**	2

Preheat oven to 375°F (190°C). Mix all filling ingredients together.

Pastry:

16 oz	**refrigerated butterflake rolls (2 tins)**	450 g

Separate butterflake biscuits, then separate individual biscuits (3–4 layers per biscuit). In greased muffin tins, arrange 2–3 flakes overlapping to form each shell. Fill with crab mixture. Bake for 8–10 minutes until puffed up and slightly browned. Serve immediately.

Gerrie Dinsley

"One day when the *Columbia* came [c. 1925], there were two young girls from the city aboard. Everyone went to Hallidays' for dinner and after it was over the girls lighted up cigarettes, a habit just then being taken up by women. The girls offered one to Mrs. Halliday. She put on her haughtiest air—'I'd rather commit adultery than smoke a cigarette,' she said in a scathing tone. 'Who wouldn't,' murmured one of the girls."

Edith Cadwallader

Broiled Prawns with Garlic Butter

Serves 6

2 lbs	**uncooked prawns in shells**	900 g

Shell prawns, leaving fan of tails intact.

6 Tbsp	**butter**	90 mL
⅓ cup	**olive oil**	75 mL
1 Tbsp	**lemon juice**	15 mL
¼ cup	**chopped shallots**	50 mL
1 Tbsp	**minced garlic**	15 mL
1 tsp	**salt**	5 mL
	freshly ground pepper to taste	

In a flameproof baking dish or pan (just large enough to hold prawns in one layer), melt butter over low heat. Stir in olive oil, lemon juice, shallots, garlic, salt and a few grindings of pepper. Add prawns and turn in butter and oil until they glisten. Place 4–5" from broiler and broil for 3–4 minutes. Turn prawns over and broil 3–4 minutes longer, just until firm and white (don't overcook).

4 Tbsp	**chopped fresh parsley**	50 mL
	fresh lemon wedges	

To serve: transfer prawns to a heated serving platter or individual heated scallop shells. Pour sauce over prawns, sprinkle with parsley and garnish with lemon.

1	**loaf French bread**	1

Pass the French bread to sop up the delicious juice!

Jacquie Gordon

Quick Shrimp Spread

Makes about 1½ cups (375 mL)

8 oz	**cream cheese,**	225 g
	at room temperature	

Place the block of cream cheese on a shallow dish or plate with a raised lip.

½ cup	**chili sauce**	125 mL
1 Tbsp	**Worcestershire sauce**	15 mL
1 Tbsp	**finely grated onion**	15 mL
1½ tsp	**lemon juice**	7 mL

Mix chili, Worcestershire sauce, onion and lemon juice together and pour over cream cheese.

6 oz	**shrimp, fresh cooked or canned**	200 g
	finely chopped fresh parsley to taste	

If using canned shrimp, rinse and drain thoroughly. Sprinkle shrimp over sauce. Sprinkle parsley over shrimp. Serve with assorted crackers.

Fran Preston

Ladies' log rolling contest at the Loggers Sports Day, Campbell River, 1950s. CRM 518.

Spinach Dip

Makes about 3 cups (750 mL)
Chill overnight

Filling:

10 oz	**frozen spinach,** thawed and well drained	300 g
8 oz	**water chestnuts, chopped**	227 mL
1	**green onion, chopped**	1
1½ cups	**sour cream**	375 mL
1 cup	**mayonnaise** (not salad dressing)	250 mL
1 pkg	**dried vegetable soup mix**	1 pkg

Chop spinach very finely. Mix in all remaining ingredients. Refrigerate overnight to marry flavours.

1	**loaf sourdough bread, round** (optional)	1

Hollow out centre of loaf and place spinach mixture in bread bowl. Cut bread into chunks and dip in sauce. Or place dip in an ordinary bowl and serve as a dip or spread for toast or crackers.

Doris Korsa

Curried Shrimp in Papaya

Serves 8

4	**papayas**	4
	lemon juice	
	fresh shrimp	

Cut papayas in half, remove seeds and sprinkle with lemon juice. Cook enough shrimp to fill papaya halves when combined with sauce.

Sauce:

4	**slices bacon, chopped**	4
¼ cup	**thinly sliced celery**	50 mL
¼ cup	**chopped onion**	50 mL
½	**garlic clove, minced**	½
2 Tbsp	**vegetable oil**	30 mL

Sauté bacon, celery, onion and garlic in oil for about 10 minutes.

¼ cup	**flour**	50 mL

Sprinkle in flour and cook mixture over low heat, stirring frequently, for another 5 minutes.

½ cup	**applesauce**	125 mL
¼ cup	**curry powder**	50 mL
3 Tbsp	**tomato paste**	45 mL
1 Tbsp	**sugar**	15 mL
1 Tbsp	**lemon juice**	15 mL
2	**beef bouillon cubes**	2
1¼ cups	**water**	300 mL
	salt to taste	

Add remaining sauce ingredients and cook over low heat for 45 minutes. If the sauce is not to be used at once, it can be cooked to this point and either refrigerated or frozen.

1 cup	**milk or light cream**	250 mL

To serve: combine 1 cup (250 mL) of the curry sauce with 1 cup (250 mL) milk or cream. Add cooked shrimp, heat through, and mound into papaya halves.

	chopped fresh parsley to taste	

Garnish with parsley.
Cooked and cubed meat, poultry or any seafood may be substituted for the shrimp in this recipe, and may be served over rice instead of papaya.

Jacque Mielke

Nancy and Tom Roberts, early pioneers of Roberts Creek, BC. In order to market produce from their small farm, Tom used to row out in a small skiff loaded with crated eggs and fruit to flag down Vancouver-bound steamships.

Smoked Salmon Pâté

Makes about 2 cups (500 mL)

8 oz	**smoked salmon**	225 g
1	**small onion**	1

In food processor, blend salmon and onion.

8 oz	**low-fat cream cheese**	225 g
¼ cup	**mayonnaise**	50 mL
2 tsp	**lemon juice**	10 mL
1 tsp	**Worcestershire sauce**	5 mL
2 tsp	**horseradish**	10 mL

Add remaining ingredients and process until blended. This easy spread can be served with an assortment of breads and crackers; excellent with Melba toast rounds. Keep refrigerated.

Jackie MacNaughton

"It was pretty crude in the old days. I was on a packer in Glendale Cove in 1922. One day I took two scows out. They'd call them 'twenty thousand scows'—they'd hold twenty thousand pinks. I took the scows to the end of the Inlet and a gang of factory workers threw them overboard. They were too rotten to can."

Jim Henderson, *CRM aural history. Henderson was a pioneer in coastal commercial fishing who lived in Campbell River for most of his life. The son of a Scots father and a Kwakwaka'wakw mother, Jim was brother to the noted First Nations artist Sam Henderson.*

Fish splitter at Rivers Inlet cannery contemplates his task. BCARS 62447.

Curried Salmon Cocktail Puffs

Makes 3–4 dozen puffs

Shells:

½ cup	**butter**	125 mL
1 cup	**boiling water**	250 mL

Preheat oven to 400°F (200°C).
In medium saucepan, heat butter with boiling water until butter is melted. Turn heat to low.

1 cup	**flour**	250 mL
½ tsp	**salt**	2 mL

Add flour and salt, stirring vigorously until mixture forms a smooth ball. Remove from heat.

4	**eggs**	4

Add eggs one at a time, beating well with a spoon after each addition. Drop by teaspoonfuls onto lightly greased cookie sheet. Bake for 20–25 minutes or until golden. Cool, split in half. Shells can be made ahead of time and frozen.

Filling:

7½ oz	**canned salmon**	213 g
⅓ cup	**mayonnaise**	75 mL
1 tsp	**curry powder, or to taste**	5 mL
2 Tbsp	**chopped green onion**	30 mL
	salt and pepper to taste	

Combine all filling ingredients and fill puffs, replacing tops. Heat before serving.

Gloria Cameron

"The Manhousat people considered barnacles at their best during the summer months, when the sea water was warmer … Pit-cooking involved lighting a fire in a pit that had been lined with black rocks, which had less tendency to crack when heated. When the fire had burned down, the hotter ashes were removed. Barnacles were stacked on top of the hot stones, and the pit was covered with a red cedar bark mat. Then a small quantity of water was added to the pit. The barnacles cooked quickly and after removal from the pit, a small stick was inserted through the mouth of each one to push out the edible insides."

Luke Swan and David Ellis,
Teachings of the Tides

Salmon Dill Pâté

Makes one 6-cup (1.5 L) mold
Chill 4 hours

1 pkg	**unflavoured gelatin**	1 pkg
¼ cup	**cold water**	50 mL

In a saucepan, soften gelatin in cold water for 10 minutes.

10 oz	**condensed tomato soup**	284 mL
8 oz	**cream cheese**	225 g

Add tomato soup and cream cheese to gelatin. Cook on low heat, whisking until smooth. Remove from heat.

1 cup	**mayonnaise**	250 mL
¾ cup	**chopped dill pickles**	175 mL
½ cup	**chopped celery or green pepper**	125 mL
¼ cup	**chopped green onion**	50 mL
7½ oz	**canned salmon**	213 g

Add remaining ingredients. Beat well. Turn into an oiled 6-cup (1.5 L) mold. Chill 4 hours or overnight, until firm. Unmold and serve with assorted crackers.

Gloria Cameron

Clam & Cheese Dip

Makes about 1 cup (250 mL)

5 oz	**canned clams**	142 g
¼ cup	**clam juice**	50 mL
6 oz	**cream cheese**	200 g
2 tsp	**chopped fresh chives or green onion**	10 mL
¼ tsp	**salt**	1 mL
1 tsp	**Worcestershire sauce**	5 mL
3 drops	**Tabasco sauce**	3 drops
1 Tbsp	**lemon juice**	15 mL
5	**fresh parsley sprigs**	5

Blend all ingredients until smooth, using a spatula as necessary. Great with raw veggies.

Joan Richards

Some women who immigrated to the coast of British Columbia adapted very well to the coastal environment and the lifestyle it provided. For those who loved the robust outdoors life and could afford to savour its pleasures, northern Vancouver Island was a paradise.

Mary (Pidcock) Smith was held up as a shining example of the ideal coastal woman in the *The Log*, the Columbia Coast Mission newsletter, of 1907. In addition to describing her superb domestic accomplishments, the author said: "Mary Smith is a typical woman of the West, able to turn her hand to anything; can handle a boat and tackle the most lively of Campbell River salmon. She is a first class shot and the finest buck of last season fell before her unerring aim."

from Silent Partners,
CRM women's history video

"A typical woman of the West," Mary (Pidcock) Smith was the daughter of early settlers at Quathiaski Cove. Her father taught all his seven children to be crack shots as soon as they could handle guns. CRM 10780.

Oyster Scallop

Serves 8

½ cup	**butter**	125 mL
½ cup	**flour**	125 mL
1½ tsp	**paprika**	7 mL
¼ tsp	**salt**	1 mL
dash	**cayenne pepper**	dash

Preheat oven to 400°F (200°C). Melt butter in heavy skillet. Add flour and cook until light brown. Stir in seasonings and cook another 3 minutes.

1	**onion, chopped fine**	1
1	**green pepper, chopped**	1
½	**garlic clove, minced**	½

Add vegetables and cook together until limp, about 10 minutes.

4 cups	**fresh shucked oysters and juice**	900 mL
1 tsp	**lemon juice**	5 mL
1 Tbsp	**Worcestershire sauce**	15 mL
	bread crumbs to taste	

"We look forward to our earliest Spring rite. This is a gathering of oysters. What we look for is an ebb tide that will drop at least ten metres. Only then will the plump cold-water oysters of our favourite bed be accessible. These are shellfish of surpassing quality.

The gathering is only part of our Spring ritual. There is also the preparing and eating. Other prerequisites are a crackling blaze in the fireplace against the chill of approaching evening and a good wine."

Arthur "Bill" Mayse

Author, journalist and scriptwriter Arthur Mayse knew and loved the coast all his life. Known as "Bill" Mayse to his many friends, he lived with his wife Win for many years in a former float house at Stories Beach, Campbell River.

Cut up big oysters and simmer all oysters 5 minutes in own juice. Stir in lemon juice and Worcestershire, add all to vegetables and mix well.

Pour into a greased 8" (20 cm) baking dish and sprinkle with bread crumbs.

Bake for 35–40 minutes or until bubbling. Serve on rye bread.

The scallop can be made ahead and refrigerated or frozen until ready to bake. Waits well over a warming candle.

Individual appetizer: Place on 8–10 greased oyster shells and sprinkle with crumbs. Bake for 10–15 minutes. Garnish.

Heather Gordon Murphy

Bunkhouse Beef Stick

Makes five 1-lb (450 g) rolls
Refrigerate 24 hours

5 lbs	**hamburger** (the fatter the better)	2 kg
3 Tbsp	**curing salt**	45 mL
2½ tsp	**black pepper**	12 mL
2½ tsp	**dried red pepper, crushed**	12 mL
2½ tsp	**mustard seeds**	12 mL
2½ tsp	**dried onion flakes**	12 mL
2½ tsp	**dried sweet basil**	12 mL
2½ tsp	**dried oregano**	12 mL
2½ tsp	**garlic powder**	12 mL

Preheat oven to 350°F (180°C).

Combine all ingredients and mix well with hands. Divide into five parts. Make each part into a roll 2" (5 cm) thick. Roll each one in a double thickness of tinfoil, sealing seams tightly. Press out as much air as possible. Twist ends tight. Refrigerate rolls for 24 hours.

Place on a rimmed cookie sheet to catch juices. Bake for 30 minutes. Reduce heat to 325°F (160°C) and bake another 45 minutes. Open one end of each roll and drain out all juices. Let cool. After removing from foil, wrap rolls in plastic wrap. Refrigerate. Slice and serve. The cooked beef stick freezes well.

Gerrie Dinsley

bunkhouse Sundays
in the windy lonesome wilderness
relieved by the toothless wit
of the camp comic
who knew every dirty joke there
was
and a few more.

Peter Trower,
"Between the Sky and the
Splinters"

In the early years of the logging
industry, bunkhouses offered only
the most basic accommodation.
Men carried their own blanket rolls
from camp to camp.
CRM 13312.

Photo taken at Sunnyside, the Yeatman farm on Quadra Island, from Rob Yeatman's photo album. CRM 6269.

"The Petersens had a big milk farm across from the Quinsam Hotel. They used to supply all of Campbellton with milk. Our milkman at Campbell River was Mr. Holmstrom. He used to bring milk down to the Bee Hive Cafe and Ice Cream Parlour which is still in business near its original location and pour it into our own containers. Finally, he got bottles."
Gwen Telosky,
CRM aural history.
In 1925, when she was fifteen years old, Gwen Telosky came to Campbell River. She worked as a cook and housekeeper for local families, waitressed in the first Bee Hive Cafe, and was a logging camp cook.

Spring Rolls

Makes 10 rolls

3½ oz	**uncooked chicken or pork, minced**	100 g
3 Tbsp	**grated carrot**	45 mL
1	**green onion, chopped**	1
2 tsp	**soy sauce**	10 mL

Combine meat, carrot, onion and soy sauce in a frying pan and cook until done.

10	**spring roll wraps**	10
¾ cup	**Mae Pranom dipping sauce for chicken** (available at Asian food stores)	175 mL

Divide meat mixture among 10 spring roll wraps. Wrap each roll, using a little flour to seal the edges. Deep-fry or pan-fry in a wok, two at a time. Serve with Mae Pranom sauce.

Jeanne Ralston

Cheese & Onion Slice

Makes one 8" (20 cm) pie

1	**recipe pastry** (two-crust)	1

Place a layer of pastry on the bottom of a shallow pie plate.

finely chopped onion
grated cheese
salt and pepper to taste
milk

Preheat oven to 350°F (180°C). Spread a layer of onion on the crust, add a layer of grated cheese and repeat until filling reaches ½'' (1 cm) below edge of pie plate. Season and pour on enough milk to moisten. Cover with pastry and bake 50 minutes or until done.

For all ingredients, use quantities to taste. This is one of those old-time recipes with imprecise directions, upon which each cook places an individual stamp—often with wonderful results.

Margaret Morris

Spring Rolls in Peanut Sauce

Serves any number

rice paper sheets	
rice vermicelli	

Filling:

grated carrot

shredded lettuce or bean sprouts

cooked shrimp or shredded cooked chicken or pork

chopped green onion

For all ingredients, use quantities to taste.

Immerse rice paper in warm water until soft, about 1 minute. Place on a tea towel. Cook vermicelli as per package instructions.

Combine all filling ingredients. Place some vermicelli and 1 Tbsp (15 mL) of filling in centre of each rice paper sheet. Fold half the rice paper over, fold in both ends and roll. You end up with a finger food roll about ½ x3" (1x7.5 cm).

	Peanut Sauce:	
½ cup	**milk**	125 mL
½ cup	**chicken stock**	125 mL
¼ cup	**peanut butter**	50 mL
1 tsp	**soy sauce**	5 mL
½	**garlic clove, pressed**	½

Combine all ingredients and simmer 10 minutes. Serve the sauce in individual containers and dip the rolls into sauce. A very attractive appetizer or lunch food.

Faye Skuse

Jalapeno Jelly

Makes about 4 cups (1 L)

¼ cup	chopped pickled jalapeno peppers	50 mL
¾ cup	chopped red pepper	175 mL
1 cup	vinegar	250 mL
3 Tbsp	lemon juice	45 mL
4 cups	sugar	900 mL
3 oz	pectin	90 g

Put jalapenos and red pepper into blender. Add half the vinegar and blend until smooth. Pour into a large saucepan. Add the remaining vinegar, lemon juice, and sugar. Bring to boil, stirring often. Boil for 10 minutes.

Add pectin and return to full rolling boil. Boil 1 minute. Remove from heat and skim.

Pour into sterilized jars and seal with paraffin as desired. The jelly will keep unsealed in the fridge for several weeks. To serve: spread crackers with cream cheese and top with jelly, or pour jelly over cream cheese brick.

June Weatherstone

❚❚ I went to work for the Thulins, delivering milk in a horse and buggy all around town. I milked sixteen or seventeen dairy cows. The barn used to be where the Tidemark Theatre now is. I used to wash the milk bottles, fill them and deliver the milk. This was about 1928–29. The bottles had 'STRATHCONA DAIRY, CAMPBELL RIVER' printed on them."

Jack Phillips,
CRM aural history.
Phillips has lived in Campbell River since 1927, when he worked for the pioneering Thulin family at the Willows Hotel.

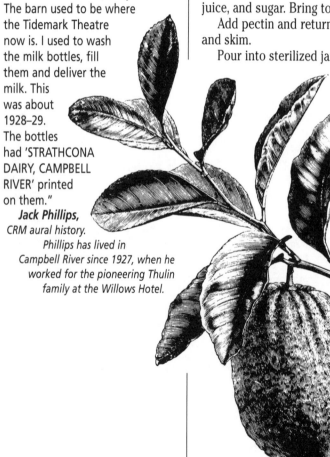

Olive Nuggets

Serves 4

¼ cup	**butter**	50 mL
1 cup	**grated sharp cheddar cheese**	250 mL
¾ cup	**flour**	175 mL
	green stuffed olives	
	paprika or poppy seeds	

Preheat oven to 350°F (180°C).

Mix the butter, cheese and flour together to make a dough. Pat olives dry and roll dough around each one, about the size of a teaspoon. Place on a cookie sheet and bake for 15–20 minutes. Sprinkle with paprika or poppy seeds. Serve warm. You can also make them ahead and reheat just before serving.

Gerrie Dinsley

Gold

While Vancouver Island was still a crown colony, prospectors used Indian canoes and trading schooners to reach inaccessible areas. The Zeballos River was discovered to be gold bearing and Zeballos was the site of a boom in the 1830s. Other gold bearing waters in the area are the Gold and the Oyster Rivers.

Gold seekers have worked the Oyster River for over one hundred years, not getting rich but making wages. One up-to-date miner uses a scuba outfit to suction sand in deep pools.

Guide and guest in a dugout, ready to go salmon fishing at Campbell River in August 1904. CRM 10215.

Pickled Chanterelle Mushrooms

Makes 6 pints (3 L)

2 cups	cider vinegar	500 mL
1 cup	vegetable oil	250 mL
2	whole garlic cloves	2
14 oz	tomato sauce	398 mL
2 Tbsp	sugar	30 mL
1 Tbsp	dried tarragon	15 mL
1	bay leaf	1

Place first seven ingredients in a large pot and bring to a boil.

3 qts	chanterelles, blanched	3 L
	strips of green bell pepper, to taste	

Add chanterelles and pepper, return to a boil, then simmer 25 minutes. Remove bay leaf.

	chilies (optional)	

Sterilize 6 1-pint (450-mL) jars. Add a chili to each jar and process in boiling water bath for 15 minutes. Should be aged a couple of months before opening.

Ian Forbes

Wild Mushrooms

*C*auliflower Mushroom (*Sparassis radicata*), which grows at the base of firs, is very versatile. I like to dry it and crush the bits and then shake it into gravy and soups. It is also delicious fresh, cut up and fried in a little butter with salt and pepper.

Chanterelles (*Cantharellus cibarius*) are delicious and have a firm texture. A chanterelle omelette is really good. I recommend that you go easy on the onions so that you don't overpower the mushroom flavour. A little chopped red or green pepper adds colour. Another way my wife and I like chanterelles is to slice and fry them, then mix with sliced tomatoes which have been marinated with chopped fresh basil."

*Ian Forbes,
a local mushroom aficionado*

Puffballs (right) come in a number of varieties and can be quite delectable when gathered young. Overripe they become soapy and were used by Native peoples as a cleaning agent.

Pecene Paprike

Serves 4

3	**large green or red bell peppers,**	3
	hot red peppers or	
	Hungarian yellow-green peppers	

Char peppers over flame or under broiler, turning often, until skins blister and blacken. Place in plastic bag, seal and let steam ten minutes so skins will slip off easily. Peel skins, cut peppers lengthwise into strips.

3	**garlic cloves, minced**	3
	olive oil to taste (optional)	
	juice of ½ lemon, or	
	¼ cup (50 mL) vinegar, or to taste	
	salt and ground pepper to taste	

Layer peppers with garlic in a glass or ceramic bowl. Cover with oil and lemon juice and season with salt and pepper. Can be prepared up to a week ahead, covered and refrigerated. Serve at room temperature. Great with grilled meat.

Martha James

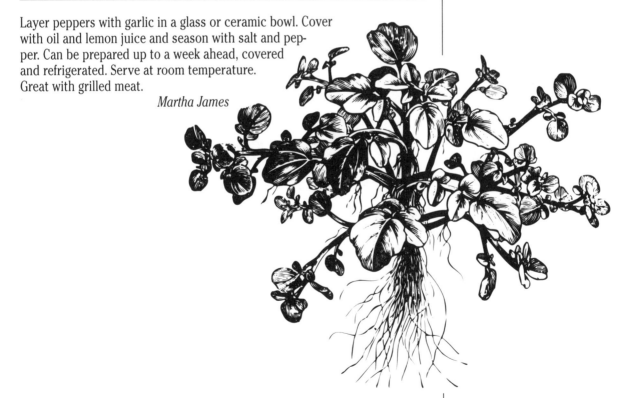

Sunday Best.
The Willson family, Quadra Island, August 1914.
(l-r) Kathleen, Cloris, Pearl, June, Grace and parents Arlette and Robert Jr.
CRM 4075

SALADS & DRESSINGS

Camp Cooks

"In the old days when I was a kid there was an awful lot of cooks in camp who were Chinese ... the tough job, you see. And the Natives, the Chinese and Japanese in the old days, in the logging camps and industry, they got all the tough jobs, where the other people didn't want it. Like all the track people ... were Japanese, usually. But there was many, many cookhouses—Chinese ... I grew up at this logging camp in Deep Bay ... and as a little boy, these Chinese used to treat us pretty nice. And I remember one little boy used to ride around in the wheelbarrow all the time with the Chinese [getting] wood for the cookhouse. And the cook would give us cookies ... There were some terrific Chinese cooks, too.

The tables, you see, there'd be all kinds of long tables in the cookhouse and ... there'd be fifteen or twenty men on each side of each table, but you never went in like a mob, you had certain manners that you catered to, and you sat in your own place, you never went to others. And if you

went to a new camp, you went into the cookhouse, you didn't go and sit down. You stood there until the head flunky came and told you where there was an empty place. And a lot of camps, the empty places, they would have a cup turned on its side. So the flunky might say, if you were a new person, 'Well, all those cups that are turned over, those are the empty

places.' It was for the good of everybody, you see. You couldn't have a madhouse—about three hundred men sitting down at once.

In big camps like that, there was a baker. And the baker, he had a helper. He'd bake all the bread and stuff and all the pies and cakes. Then you had a lunch maker you see, all the men took lunch. And the lunch maker, in those days, he would have an assistant too, because he would have tables of sandwiches, different kinds, so when you went in the morning you picked what you wanted. The flunkies, the waiters—there'd be ten or twelve of them, at least. And they had certain rules and regulations when you were at the table, too."

Ray Stockand,
CRM aural history.
Stockand, a longtime logger,
grew up in the Comox
Valley area.

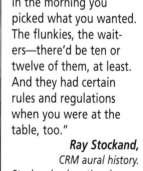

Photos: (top) UBC; (left) VPL 1592.

Cole Slaw with a Difference

Serves 6–8

4 cups	**shredded cabbage, red or green**	900 mL
1 cup	**seedless grapes, red or green**	250 mL
½ cup	**toasted almonds**	125 mL

Choose red or green cabbage and red or green grapes to complement the colour of the rest of your meal. Wash grapes and slice lengthwise. Chop almonds coarsely. Mix all salad ingredients together.

	Dressing:	
¼ tsp	**salt**	1 mL
1 tsp	**mustard powder**	5 mL
½ tsp	**grated onion, with juice**	2 mL
½ tsp	**sugar**	2 mL
⅔ cup	**mayonnaise, or**	150 mL
⅓ cup	**mayonnaise and**	75 mL
⅓ cup	**plain yoghurt**	75 mL

Blend all dressing ingredients.

Stephanie Tipple

" A truck used to come down the road. One used to sell bread and another used to sell produce."
Noel Vanstone, CRM aural history

"I can't remember the bread but the other one was a fellow, Leung, from Courtenay and he used to come up with an open sided truck with racks with all his produce on them and somebody'd yell 'Here comes the Chinaman' which is fairly racist by today's standards but that's what he was called and I can remember, of course this was wartime and one of the Perkins said, 'You got any Japanese oranges?' and of course he'd get furious."

Ramona Vanstone,
CRM aural history
The Vanstone family have lived in the Campbell River area since 1898. Pioneer logger and merchant David Vanstone contributed much to the growth and development of the area.

Broccoli Salad

Serves 6
Chill at least 2 hours

3 cups	**broccoli florets**	700 mL
½ cup	**sliced red onion**	125 mL
½ cup	**sunflower seeds**	125 mL
½ cup	**raisins**	125 mL
½ cup	**crumbled feta cheese**	125 mL

Combine all salad ingredients.

	Dressing:	
½ cup	**low-fat yoghurt**	125 mL
¼ cup	**light mayonnaise**	50 mL
2 Tbsp	**sugar**	30 mL
1 Tbsp	**lemon juice**	15 mL
	salt and pepper to taste	

Combine all dressing ingredients and pour over salad. Chill for at least 2 hours.

Jackie MacNaughton

Joe Kersey, owner of The Brigg Seafood House in Port Hardy, collects local wild foods and serves them in his restaurant. On the tidal flats in front of his restaurant in early summer, he collects what he calls sea asparagus (*Salicornia*) and serves it steamed as a vegetable or raw in his seafood salads. Archibald Menzies, Captain Vancouver's botanist, noted in 1792 that the Salish Indians used this food plant.

Broccoli and Grape Salad

Serves 10

1 cup	**seedless green grapes**	250 mL
1 cup	**seedless red grapes**	250 mL
5 cups	**broccoli florets**	1.2 L

Cut grapes in half lengthwise. Wash grapes and broccoli and lay on paper to absorb moisture.

8	**bacon slices**	8
½ cup	**finely chopped celery**	125 mL
½ cup	**finely chopped green onion**	125 mL
⅔ cup	**slivered almonds**	150 mL

Cook bacon until crisp, and crumble. Combine with all other salad ingredients.

	Dressing:	
1 cup	**mayonnaise**	250 mL
⅓ cup	**sugar**	75 mL
1 Tbsp	**vinegar**	15 mL

Combine all dressing ingredients and toss with salad.

June Wagner

Fifty years ago he cleared his land,
He respects it and tends it well.
It fed his children,
The bones of their children are
    strong.

Hubert Evans

French Potato Salad

Serves 8

Prepare 24 hours ahead

2 lbs	**red potatoes, unpeeled**	900 g

Drop whole potatoes into a large pot of boiling salted water. Bring to boil again, cover and reduce heat. Cook 7–15 minutes until tender but still firm. Leave skins on and slice while still fairly hot.

¼ cup	**chopped green onion**	50 mL
2 Tbsp	**chopped fresh parsley**	30 mL
	salt to taste	
	freshly ground pepper to taste	
2 tsp	**tarragon, dried or fresh**	10 mL

Add green onion, parsley, tarragon, salt and pepper to potatoes in a large bowl.

	Dressing:	
½ cup	**olive oil**	125 mL
¼ cup	**beef stock**	50 mL
¼ cup	**tarragon vinegar**	50 mL

Combine all dressing ingredients and gently mix with potatoes and seasonings. Cover and keep at room temperature until all dressing is absorbed. Keep in a cool place until ready to use. If refrigerated take salad out a couple of hours before use as the oil may solidify.

Gerrie Dinsley

Potatoes sold for $100 per ton so the Thulins dug up the field and planted potatoes.

Digging potatoes behind Willows Hotel, Campbell River, BC, c. 1918. Left to right: Lillie Thulin, Elin Thulin, Mrs. Carl Thulin, two unidentified men. In front of Mrs. Thulin is a Japanese gardener employed by the hotel (shown in background). The pioneering Thulin family contributed in many ways to the development of the Campbell River area. CRM 7505.

Potato Salad for a Crowd

Serves a lot!
Refrigerate overnight

24	**potatoes**	24
1 lb	**bacon**	450 g
1 qt	**garlic dill pickles, drained and chopped**	1 L
1	**large onion, finely chopped**	1

Cook, cool and slice potatoes. Cook, drain and crumble bacon. Combine bacon, chopped dills and onion and mix with potatoes.

	Dressing:	
1 cup	**mayonnaise, or** ¾ cup [175 mL] **mayonnaise and** ¼ cup [50 mL] **yoghurt**	250 mL
1 tsp	**fresh dill**	5 mL
1	**garlic clove, crushed**	1
	salt and pepper to taste	

Mix all dressing ingredients together. Toss with potatoes and refrigerate overnight.

12	**hard-boiled eggs**	12

Slice eggs and arrange on top of salad (or chop and toss with other ingredients).

	fresh dill
	paprika

Garnish with dill and paprika.

Stephanie Tipple

The Campbell River government wharf, 1915. The wharf was built in 1906. Arrivals from the boat are walking to the "Annex," a hotel owned by the Thulin brothers. CRM 6818.

" I arrived at Lourdes Hospital in Campbell River about the eighth of February in 1927. I went there to work in the kitchen. We grew our own vegetables. We had a cow and chickens. We gathered clams down in front of the hospital. The food was for the staff as well as for the patients."

Sister Angelica, *CRM aural history*
The Sisters of St. Ann administered the hospital at Campbell River from 1926 to 1957.

"**N**othing went to waste; it wasn't necessarily tradition, it was economy. If a deer had been killed, the bones were boiled up to make deer stock. Vegetable peelings were boiled up and given to the dogs."

Irene McMann,
from a conversation recorded in 1992.
Irene remembers a summer night at the upstairs window, counting the cows in the field and knowing that one was missing. It was going to be shot. Then it would be hung in the barn and skinned. The meat would sit on the table in the living room—the coolest place in the house. Then her uncle Arthur would wrap it in cheesecloth and take it down to the village at Cape Mudge to sell.
Alfred and Anna Joyce, Irene McMann's grandparents, homesteaded on Quadra Island in 1892. Irene's uncle, Arthur Joyce, was the first white boy born on Quadra—or Valdez, as it was then known.

Marinated Carrot Salad

Serves 6–8

2 lbs	**carrots, sliced**	900 g
1	**green pepper, chopped**	1
1	**medium onion, chopped**	1

Cook carrots until done but still firm. Cool and add pepper and onion.

	Marinade:	
10 oz	**condensed tomato soup**	284 mL
1 tsp	**prepared mustard**	5 mL
¼ cup	**oil**	50 mL
1 tsp	**Worcestershire sauce**	5 mL
1 cup	**sugar, or less to taste**	250 mL
½ cup	**vinegar**	125 mL
	salt and pepper to taste	

Combine all marinade ingredients and pour over vegetables. Chill. To serve: drain marinade and serve on a bed of lettuce if desired.

Jackie MacNaughton

Boat Day at Cortes Island. In the lives of coastal settlers, the arrival of a Union Steamship bringing mail, passengers and freight was always a highlight. CRM 19332.

Italian Carrot Salad

Serves 4–6

6	carrots	6
½ cup	chopped green pepper	125 mL
½ cup	chopped celery	125 mL

Steam carrots until cooked but still firm. Slice into thin pennies. Add green pepper and celery.

	Dressing:	
½ cup	**olive oil**	125 mL
¼ cup	**wine vinegar**	50 mL
2	**garlic cloves, minced**	2
1 tsp	**oregano**	5 mL
½ tsp	**cinnamon**	2 mL
4 Tbsp	**chopped fresh parsley**	50 mL
2 Tbsp	**chopped fresh dill**	30 mL
2 Tbsp	**chopped fresh mint**	30 mL

Combine all dressing ingredients and toss with vegetables.

1 cup	**fresh brown bread crumbs, pea-sized**	250 mL

Toss salad again with bread crumbs.

Ermie Iaci

Pearl, Pansy and Marion Schnarr in the tub at the August Schnarr homestead in Bute Inlet, early 1920s. CRM 14411.

"Peter Jamieson, of Aberdeen, Scotland; chief cook for the party; pride of our hearts, as well as delight of our palates ... has been a cook from boyhood. Was chef for the party that Earl Grey, Governor General of Canada, took into the Yukon and again into the Kootenays. His great avoirdupois, about two hundred and fifty pounds puts obstacles in the path of his being an explorer, but he does his best to surmount them, and has been entirely satisfactory. Our 'fat cook' is one of the features of the trip that we would not dispense with for anything.

Pete calls us to dinner, offering us vermicelli soup, lobster pâtés, mutton (canned), a la Spanish, etc., and plum pudding with proper sauce—not bad for the woods! And he has been grumbling that the packers have sent him nothing to cook or to cook with."

Harry Mc.C. Johnson,
Journal of BC Exploratory Survey Trip into the Buttle's Lake Region *(the Ellison Expedition), 1910. BCARS.*

Lettuce with Creamy Dressing

Serves 4

1	head iceberg lettuce, or other lettuce	1

Cut lettuce into large wedges.

	Dressing:	
¼ cup	light mayonnaise	50 mL
1 Tbsp	white wine vinegar	15 mL
1 Tbsp	water	15 mL
1 Tbsp	olive oil	15 mL
2 tsp	Dijon mustard	10 mL
1	garlic clove, minced	1
	salt and pepper to taste	

Whisk all dressing ingredients together and drizzle lettuce with dressing.

	basil to taste	

Sprinkle with basil and serve.

Jackie MacNaughton

Camping on the Elk River during an exploratory expedition into the Strathcona Park region by the Honorable Price Ellison and party, 1910. CRM 10119.

Sauerkraut Salad

Serves 6
Refrigerate overnight

Dressing:		
⅓ cup	**oil**	75 mL
⅓ cup	**vinegar**	75 mL

Boil oil and vinegar together. Cool.

1 cup	**sugar**	250 mL
24 oz	**sauerkraut, drained**	682 mL
1 cup	**shredded carrot**	250 mL
1 cup	**chopped green pepper**	250 mL
1 cup	**chopped celery**	250 mL
1 cup	**chopped onion**	250 mL

Combine remaining ingredients and toss with dressing. Salad will keep in the refrigerator for at least 2 weeks.

Annette Hinch

"The usual shipboard diet was salt beef, salt pork, hardtack (flour and water biscuits), peas, wheat, oatmeal, butter and cheese, sugar, olive oil, vinegar, suet, raisins, potable soup (bouillon), beer, wine grog (spirits and water), and plenty of Captain Cook's cure-all, sauerkraut.

Cook believed that the captain must eat what his people did, to keep them faithful to his nutritive regime; Vancouver doubtless believed the same. His special diet likely consisted of salad greens grown on board ship, rob (extract) of lemon and orange, marmalade of carrots, sweet wort (thickened malt solution), mustard, and fresh bread. He likely also foreswore his everyday food, most particularly sauerkraut, which may have had the best remedial effect on his mysterious, undiagnosed condition."

On Stormy Seas:
The Triumphs and
Torments of Captain George
Vancouver,
B. Guild Gillespie

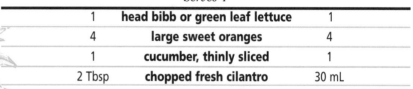

Orange Salad

Serves 4

1	**head bibb or green leaf lettuce**	1
4	**large sweet oranges**	4
1	**cucumber, thinly sliced**	1
2 Tbsp	**chopped fresh cilantro**	30 mL

Tear lettuce into bite-sized pieces. Save 1 orange for juice. Peel the other 3 oranges, remove all white pith and slice very thinly. Arrange oranges and cucumbers alternately on top of lettuce, sprinkle cilantro over all.

thinly sliced red onion rings (optional)	
raisins (optional)	

Sprinkle onion rings and raisins on top of salad if desired.

	Dressing:	
3 Tbsp	**olive oil**	45 mL
3 Tbsp	**fresh orange juice**	45 mL
1 Tbsp	**lemon juice**	15 mL
	salt and pepper to taste	
pinch	**sugar**	pinch

The Yeatman family and their friends enjoy a picnic together at Cape Mudge Light, 1902. Another pioneer recalled that the Yeatmans loved picnics.
CRM 4367.

Blend dressing ingredients. Pour over salad just before serving and toss salad at the table.

Gerrie Dinsley

Spinach & Strawberry Salad

Serves 4
Prepare dressing 1 day ahead

Dressing:		
½ cup	**berry sugar**	125 mL
	juice of 2 lemons	
2	**egg yolks**	2
¾ cup	**oil**	175 mL

Combine sugar and lemon juice, stir until dissolved. Add egg yolks and beat until creamy. Blend in oil. The dressing should be thick. Refrigerate at least 24 hours before serving.

10 oz	**fresh spinach**	283 g

Wash spinach well, dry and store in refrigerator.

⅔ cup	**pine nuts**	150 mL
24	**fresh strawberries, sliced**	24

Divide spinach among 4 individual salad plates and sprinkle with pine nuts and sliced strawberries. Whisk dressing and drizzle it over the salads.

Gerrie Dinsley

"There was a lot of fruit available. We always got a lot of apples from Quadra [Island], from Eddie Joyce for one.

When we went picking berries, that was a big thing—blackberries, saskatoons. My mom used to hang little cans around our necks and away we'd go. When we'd fill that up we'd dump it in a bigger one. She'd make lunches and we'd spend a whole day picking berries. Next day she'd be making jam, all day. We had a jam shed. It was huge—just for jam—everything: apricots, peaches, plums, blackberries, huckleberries. I still go picking berries every year. I got fourteen quarts of wild blackberries last year. I love picking. It was a good life years ago."

Bill Henderson

Nellie (Smith) Jeffrey proudly displays the outcome of a berry picking expedition.
CRM 19489.

Local and Personal

A woman whose place along this
    shore is
west of mine reports that kelp
    stalks
make a tasty pickle
but her neighbours report that
she still grows cucumbers

Hubert Evans,
Mostly Coast People

*An unidentified photo, from the
album of Myrtle (Mackenzie) Heron.
CRM uncat.*

Tarragon Tomatoes

Serves 6
Marinate overnight

6	**tomatoes, peeled and sliced**	6
1	**onion, sliced**	1
2 Tbsp	**chopped fresh parsley**	30 mL

Place tomato and onion slices in a flat dish. Sprinkle with parsley.

	Dressing:	
¼ tsp	**dry mustard**	1 mL
1 Tbsp	**sugar**	15 mL
1 cup	**tarragon vinegar**	250 mL
1 tsp	**tarragon**	5 mL
½ tsp	**cayenne**	2 mL
1	**garlic clove, crushed**	1
¾ cup	**olive oil**	175 mL

Combine dressing ingredients, shake well and pour over tomato and onion.
Keep covered and marinate overnight.

Gerrie Dinsley

Marinated Onions

Serves 4

Marinate 6–8 hours; chill 30 minutes

1 cup	**white sugar**	250 mL
1 cup	**white vinegar**	250 mL
4	**large Spanish onions**	4

Boil sugar and vinegar together for 5 minutes. Slice onions very thin and separate the rings. Pour vinegar mixture over onions and marinate 6–8 hours. Drain and pat dry with paper towels.

	Dressing:	
1 cup	**mayonnaise**	250 mL
	celery seed or dill to taste	

Toss onions with dressing. Chill for 30 minutes.

Madge Painter

Landing supplies at coastal lighthouses was a perilous job.

"Shortly before moving into the big house, John Manson built a shack on Mitlenatch Island, a small, lonely island covered with wild flowers and birds about ten miles from Cortes, and they lived there for a short time. For many years Uncle John kept sheep on Mitlenatch and he rowed them back and forth from there, two at a time, in a rowboat.

In fact, Uncle John did considerable rowing in his time. There being no road for many years Uncle John had to transport his stock, poultry feed and supplies around Reef Point, a distance of about seven miles. He used to row his butchered beef and mutton to Comox, about thirty miles, and bring back groceries. And steamship service in those days being unreliable, much as it is now, quite often logging camps would run out of meat. John and Mike had many cattle on the island which had run wild. When logging camps asked for meat they would hunt down these cattle, shoot them in the woods and dress them there. Then they had to carry the dressed meat out on their backs to the nearest beach and take it by rowboat to the camp."

from "Manson's Landing Mirror," a newspaper column dated 1957, by Peg Pyner

Thai Beef Salad

Serves 4

Marinate for 2 hours

1 lb	**flank steak**	450 g

Slice steak thinly.

	Marinade:	
¼ cup	**coriander seed**	50 mL
2 Tbsp	**garlic, minced**	30 mL
1½ tsp	**salt**	7 mL
¼ tsp	**pepper**	1 mL

Pound coriander, garlic, salt and pepper in mortar and pestle to make a paste. Spread paste over beef and marinate for 2 hours. Grill beef until done.

4	**serrano chilies**	4
1	**cucumber**	1
1	**red onion**	1
1	**head iceberg lettuce**	1

Chop chilies, slice cucumber diagonally and slice onion paper thin. Shred lettuce.

	Dressing:	
6 Tbsp	**lime juice**	90 mL
1 Tbsp	**bottled Thai fish sauce**	15 mL
2 Tbsp	**sugar**	30 mL

Mix all dressing ingredients together. To serve: arrange lettuce, beef, chilies, cucumber and onion on platter. Pour dressing over.

	chopped green onion to taste	
1 cup	**chopped fresh cilantro**	250 mL

Garnish with green onions and fresh cilantro.

Jeanne Ralston

Basil & Walnut Salad Dressing

Makes about 1¼ cups (300 mL)

1 cup	**fresh basil leaves**	250 mL
1 Tbsp	**Dijon mustard**	15 mL
⅓ cup	**red wine vinegar**	75 mL
½ tsp	**sugar**	2 mL

Process basil, mustard, vinegar and sugar in blender for 1 minute.

1 cup	**walnut oil**	250 mL
	salt and pepper to taste	

With blender running, pour in a slow stream of oil and blend for 10 seconds. Let sit for 5 minutes. Taste and adjust salt and pepper.

½ cup	**walnut pieces**	125 mL

With blender on, add the nuts. Turn off blender immediately. Nut pieces should be about the size of peppercorns and evenly chopped. Cover and refrigerate dressing until ready to use.

Jay Stewart

Part of the July 1st parade at Campbell River, 1954. The Bee Hive was a popular cafe. CRM 1862.

"As a boy, I was always interested in insects. I learned bee-keeping from Tom Broadland and Bob Hartt. Tom helped me for the first eight to ten years; I've been keeping bees for thirty years.

As time went on, I made a bit of money from keeping bees. I had three hundred and fifty colonies at most. The average production is one hundred pounds per hive per season.

The main crop is fireweed which grows on the clear-cuts. I also sell dandelion, maple and salal honey.

In the spring I put my hives out at thirteen sites in the woods, from Oyster River to Sayward and west to Buttle [Lake]. You have to have good weather for the bees to produce. They can't work in the fog.

There are ten bee-keepers on the Island who have made a living at it. It only works because of the logging."

George "Honey" Brown

Honey Mustard Dressing

Makes about 1¼ cups (425 mL)

1 tsp	**dry mustard**	5 mL
1 tsp	**salt**	5 mL
2 tsp	**celery seed**	10 mL
⅓ cup	**white vinegar or white wine vinegar**	75 mL
1 Tbsp	**grated onion**	15 mL
½ cup	**honey**	125 mL

Combine mustard, salt and celery seed and place in blender. Add vinegar, onions and honey.

1 cup	**vegetable oil**	250 mL

With blender running, gradually add oil.

Carol Brown

Herb Salad Dressing

Makes 1 cup (250 mL)

1 tsp	**finely chopped fresh parsley**	5 mL
1 tsp	**finely chopped fresh basil**	5 mL
1 tsp	**minced fresh tarragon**	5 mL
1 tsp	**minced fresh chervil**	5 mL
2	**garlic cloves, minced**	2

Mix herbs and garlic together.

2 Tbsp	**fresh lemon juice**	30 mL
2 Tbsp	**wine vinegar**	30 mL
1 Tbsp	**Dijon mustard**	15 mL

Add lemon juice and vinegar to mustard, then add herb mixture. Mix well.

¾ cup	**olive oil**	175 mL

While whisking dressing constantly, add oil in steady stream until all is blended.

dash	**Tabasco sauce**	dash
	salt and pepper to taste	

Add remaining ingredients and mix well.

Estelle Inman

Floathouses

"Upon a gathering of enormous rafts of cedar logs a cluster of houses lay. Though made up of sections, the whole was held together by boom chains and cable, presenting to the viewer an air of compactness, a community stability, that certain something one senses only in established places. Ridiculous as this impression seemed regarding a so obviously transient arrangement, the feeling grew stronger upon me as I stepped upon the planking of the City.

I started along the main street of this astonishing floating aggregation of one-storey buildings. All were of frame, from one to five rooms in size. Several were of tar-paper covering, others of cedar shakes, others of neat boards.

In little yards at the front and back of these flowers and vegetables flourished in earth held in old dugout canoes, long boxes, barrels and tins.

From the nearby shore pipelines, tapping mountain springs, had been carried to supply the householders with running water."

Francis Dickie, *CRM archives Dickie lived at Heriot Bay on Quadra Island and published magazine and newspaper articles during the 1920s and 1930s.*

The Reynolds' float at Claydon Bay, 1939. In the 1940s, Claydon Bay was one of the most highly developed of the floating villages. Francis Barrow, who spent many summers travelling the coast, recorded a "warm welcome" here. CRM 14141.

The Kelly Logging Company cookhouse
at Church Creek.
CRM 3947

SOUPS & CHOWDERS

Camp Life in the Old Days

"In those days, there was three hundred men sat down at once in the cookhouse. They rang the bell and you all went running into the cookhouse. And the cook—there'd be a cook, a second cook and a bunch of kitchen mechanics—they were the

potato peelers and dishwashers—then the flunkies on the tables, and all that sort of thing. In those old-fashioned camps if you had a good cook, he was like God. That's a pretty important job.

And you had certain manners. When you went into the cookhouse you sat in your own place, and you said 'please' and 'thank you,' and you didn't reach in front of people and all that sort of thing—there were certain manners. And these new people, that had never been in camp before, they'd stand out like a—absolutely different. 'Course, I say some of those guys come into camp—skid row boys—when they saw all that food, they'd go crazy. But anyway, the dif-

ference is now ... they have a contract caterer ... All these young people they go crying to him, they want this and that, and he's trying to please them. And I say to these guys, they don't know how lucky they are. Christ Almighty. I know one camp I went to they wanted Kool-Aid. I said, 'Kool-Aid!? What the hell does a logger

want Kool-Aid for? You're supposed to have liquor and stuff.' And then they open a bottle of liquor, and a week later they got the same bottle. And they drink it in front of ya (without sharing it, as was customary before) ... Times are sure different.

Here's one of the stories about the old-fashioned cookhouses ... These two management loggers they meet each other in Vancouver—this is the old days, you see. One

guys says, 'How did you do last year on your logging?' The guy says, 'Oh, I didn't make any money loggin' but I made $10,000 on the cookhouse.' You see, you had to pay your board. They used to charge you $1.50 a day board. And a cook—the management would try and get him to be cheaper and cheaper, so they could make money, and of course the men are after him for better food ...

I know when I was up at the lighthouse I used to make pies and things when I felt like it. And this old native Indian next door used to come and visit. I just made pies one day and he was tickled to death at the pies and he said to me, 'Why don't you get a job cookin' in a loggin' camp?' I said, 'Don't be crazy, that's the worst bloody job there is! You're first person up, you're the last person in bed, you got the men all after you, you got the management all after you. Seven days a week. That's the worst job of all.'"

Ray Stockand, a logger who grew up in the Comox Valley area, CRM aural history
Photo: VPL 1688

Cheddar Potato & Onion Soup

Serves 4–5

3	**medium onions, diced**	3
2 Tbsp	**butter**	30 mL

In a soup pot, sauté onion in butter until soft.

4	**potatoes, cubed**	4
2 cups	**chicken stock**	500 mL
4	**shakes of black pepper**	4
¼ tsp	**basil**	1 mL
¼ tsp	**dill**	1 mL
¼ tsp	**salt**	1 mL

Add potatoes, stock and seasonings. Cover and bring to a soft boil. Reduce heat and simmer gently for 25 minutes or until potatoes are soft. Remove pot from stove, blend contents until smooth.

3 cups	**milk**	700 mL
1 cup	**grated medium cheddar cheese**	250 mL

Return pot to stove and toss in milk and cheese. Reheat slowly until cheese is totally absorbed. Do not boil!

Bruce Saunders

"Of the sea animals, the most common that we saw in use amongst them, as food, is the porpoise; the fat or rind of which, as well as the flesh, they cut in large pieces, and having dried them, as they do the herrings, eat them without any farther preparation. They also prepare a sort of broth from this animal, in its fresh state, in a singular manner, putting pieces of it in a square wooden vessel or bucket, with water, and then throwing heated stones into it. This operation they repeat till they think the contents are sufficiently stewed or seethed. They put in the fresh, and take out the other stones, with a cleft stick, which serves as tongs; the vessel being always placed near the fire, for that purpose. This is a pretty common dish amongst them; and, from its appearance, seems to be strong, nourishing food. The oil which they procure from these and other sea animals, is also used by them in great quantities; both supping it alone, with a large scoop or spoon, made of horn or mixing it with other food, as sauce."

Capt. James Cook, A Voyage to the Pacific Ocean, 1776–1778

The oil used by many Natives came from a small sardine-like fish known as the eulachon.
Hubert Evans photo.

The Willows Hotel

" **I**n the early days, after 1904, our first hotel was overcrowded, so we had to build a new hotel. The second hotel burned so we had to build a third hotel. It opened July 1, 1909. It was very notable and popular. We had a large number of tourists and in the summer we had six to eight waitresses. It was noted very much for the board. We had a lot of notable tourists. A good number were ex-English army officers."

Carl Thulin Sr., CRM aural history
The original Willows Hotel was built by the Thulin brothers in 1904 and boomed with business from loggers and fishermen. A larger hotel was built but burned shortly after completion. The "third" Willows Hotel was then constructed and the first hotel became the "Annex." The Willows Hotel was a landmark in Campbell River until it too was destroyed by fire in 1963. The Thulin family also built a general store in the Campbell River area.

The Campbell River waterfront, c. 1912. The Willows Hotel is at left. CRM 4203.

Cheddar & Vegetable Soup

Serves 6

1	**large carrot, diced**	1
2	**celery stalks, diced**	2
1	**onion, chopped**	1
½	**green pepper, diced**	½
¼ cup	**butter**	50 mL

In a large saucepan, sauté all vegetables in butter until soft.

⅓ cup	**flour**	75 mL
4 cups	**chicken broth**	900 mL

Stir in flour and cook for 3 minutes, stirring constantly. Add chicken broth and bring to a boil, stirring constantly. Simmer uncovered for 15 minutes. Remove from heat.

⅓ lb	**sharp cheddar cheese, grated**	150 g
2 cups	**milk**	500 mL

Stir in cheese and milk. Gently reheat but do not allow to boil. Serve hot.

Vera de Haas

Corn Chowder

Serves 2–4

	seaweed to taste	
14 oz	**corn and juice**	398 mL
	eulachon oil to taste	

Combine all ingredients and heat just until hot. If desired you can add eulachon oil to individual servings rather than to the pot of chowder.

Daisy Price

"We used to go out sometime in May to the island and gather seaweed from the rocks. According to the old Indian people it was really good when it had only grown five to six inches long. It was quite dark and flat and we just pulled it off the rocks at low tide and laid it on some screens made of cedar wood to dry it out. Sometimes we would roast it in the oven and then just smash it up so that it was just like tobacco. Sometimes we would eat it plain or boil it mixed with fish eggs or mix it with clams or dip it in olachen oil."

Guests Never Leave Hungry, The Autobiography of James Sewid, a Kwakiutl Indian, ed. James P. Spradley

James Sewid *was born at Alert Bay in 1913 and died in Campbell River in 1988. He was both a hereditary and an elected chief, and he was active in reviving Native traditions.*

71

Tomato Soup

Serves 8–10

2 cups	**diced raw potatoes**	500 mL
¾ cup	**minced onion**	175 mL
1 cup	**coarsely chopped celery**	250 mL
3 cups	**skinned, chopped tomato**	700 mL
2 tsp	**salt, or less to taste**	10 mL
¼ tsp	**pepper**	1 mL
¼ tsp	**oregano**	1 mL
2½ cups	**water**	625 mL

Boil first eight ingredients until tender and saucelike in consistency.

	Sauce:	
3 Tbsp	**butter**	45 mL
¼ cup	**flour**	50 mL
1½ tsp	**salt**	7 mL
¼ tsp	**pepper**	1 mL
½ tsp	**dry mustard**	2 mL
2 cups	**milk**	500 mL
1 tsp	**Worcestershire sauce**	5 mL

Make a roux from the butter and flour. Add remaining sauce ingredients. Add cooked vegetables and simmer 15 minutes.

1½ cups	**grated cheddar cheese**	375 mL
	chopped fresh parsley to taste	

Add cheese and parsley to soup.

1 tsp	**sugar** (optional)	5 mL

Taste soup and add sugar if tomatoes are too acid.

Doris Korsa

The Willson family of Quadra Island, August 1914. Robert Willson Jr. (seated) homesteaded on Quadra, then known as Valdes Island, c. 1893. CRM 3889.

Fagioli Soup

Serves 7–8

1 lb	**bacon, diced**	450 g
2	**onions, coarsely chopped**	2
28 oz	**canned whole Italian plum tomatoes with juice**	796 mL
28 oz	**water**	796 mL

In a 5–6 qt (5–6 L) saucepan, fry bacon and onions until tender. Add tomatoes, including all the juice, and water.

2	**14 oz (398 mL) tins white kidney beans**	2
1 tsp	**basil**	5 mL
1 tsp	**rosemary**	5 mL
1½ tsp	**oregano**	7 mL
1 tsp	**marjoram**	5 mL
1 tsp	**coarse black pepper**	5 mL

Drain beans and discard liquid. Add beans to pot. Add herbs and pepper and stir thoroughly but gently so the tomatoes remain whole. Bring to a soft boil and turn down heat. Partially cover and simmer 2 hours, or until volume is reduced by one quarter.

dry red wine (optional)	

If the soup is too thick, add a splash of dry red wine and a bit of water.

Bruce Saunders

Salt Pork and Firehole Beans

" In the early years logging bunkhouses were primitive, salt pork and firehole beans were the daily fare and the hardest of hard labour was expected from the men. A man packed his own blanket roll or 'bindle' from camp to camp. On some shows, the standard measure of a 'tame ape's' worth was whether he could hoist a barrel of salt pork to his shoulders. As the industry developed the bunkhouses became more comfortable."
a museum label written by the late Arthur Mayse, to accompany a photograph of a typical camp bunkhouse

Delicious Oyster Soup

Serves 3

2½ cups	**light cream**	625 mL
10 oz	**oysters, fresh poached or canned**	284 mL
¼ cup	**cooked spinach**	50 mL
2 Tbsp	**butter**	30 mL
1	**garlic clove, minced**	
1½ tsp	**A1 steak sauce**	7 mL
½ tsp	**salt**	2 mL
½ tsp	**pepper**	2 mL
dash	**cayenne**	dash

In a large pot, heat cream to simmer. Purée oysters in blender and add to cream. Purée spinach in blender and add to cream. Add butter, garlic, steak sauce, salt, pepper and cayenne to simmering cream. Heat again to simmer, whisking until smooth. Do not boil.

2 tsp	**cornstarch**	10 mL
2 tsp	**water**	10 mL

In a separate container, mix cornstarch with water. Add cornstarch mixture to soup. Heat and whisk until soup is slightly thickened. Taste to adjust seasonings.

⅔ cup	**whipping cream** (optional)	150 mL

Whip the cream. Ladle soup into bowls and top each serving with a spoonful of whipped cream. Slip under broiler until cream is well glazed and brown.

Jackie MacNaughton

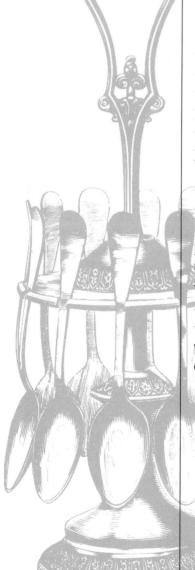

Manhattan Clam Chowder

Serves 6–8

6	slices bacon, chopped	6
1 cup	chopped onion	250 mL
½ cup	chopped green pepper	125 mL
⅔ cup	chopped celery	150 mL

Sauté bacon. Add onion, pepper and celery. Cook just until tender.

1 tsp	thyme	5 mL
1	clove garlic, minced	1
	salt and pepper to taste	
3 cups	diced potatoes	750 mL
4 cups	clamato juice	900 mL
2 cups	diced carrots	500 mL
1 cup	chopped tomatoes, fresh or canned	250 mL
1	bay leaf, crumbled	1
2 Tbsp	sugar	30 mL
dash	Worcestershire sauce	dash
2 Tbsp	chopped fresh parsley	30 mL
dash	Tabasco sauce	dash

Add remaining ingredients and simmer 1 hour.

3 cups	chopped clams, canned or fresh	750 mL

If using canned clams, add clams and juice, and simmer 30 minutes. If using fresh clams, steam them in shell until done, then chop and add to soup, simmer 1 hour.

	chopped fresh parsley	

Serve garnished with parsley.

Gerrie Dinsley

" After considerable dickering, and by signs and gestures and words oft repeated we were able to impart the information that we wanted her ... to 'show us how to cook the clams and that we would buy some.' This brought some merriment in the camp. The idea, that there lived a person that did not know how to cook clams."

Ezra Meeker,
Pioneer Reminiscences of Puget Sound

Clam Chowder the Traditional Way

This traditional preparation was taught to me by my father, one of the pioneering Pidcocks at Quathiaski Cove.

Don gumboots and warm clothing. Armed with shovel and pail, make for a clam bed at low tide. Butter clams thrive in sand-gravel beaches mainly in the lower third of the tidal range, where they may be found at least 12" (30.5 cm) deep. Unlike oysters, clams are at their best when preparing to spawn in summer, and at their least tasty immediately after spawning. Dig up a bucketful, wash them and drop into your pail of sea water. If the clam is fat, its shells may not be tightly closed. Take home and set pail in a cool place, after sprinkling oatmeal into it to deal with any sand.

Ready to make clam chowder?

In a large pot, sauté ½ cup (125 mL) chopped bacon until fat is clear. Add 1 cup (250 mL) diced onion, 2 cups (500 mL) diced potato and sufficient water to boil the mixture.

Above a large bowl, open clams with a dull knife cutting through the muscles on either side of the clam's hinge. Open each clam using the knife to loosen the clam from its shells. Drop into the bowl in order to keep all the clam liquor. Pull away the clam's spout (or siphon) and the attached membrane and discard. If desired, chop up clam into smaller pieces and return to bowl.

When potatoes are done, add clams and set pot on a low boil for no more than 10–15 minutes. Then add a large tin of evaporated milk, reheat and serve. Of course amounts may be varied to taste. I often add celery and thyme.

A satisfying meal for a cold stormy day.

Ruth Barnett

Campbell River in the early 1940s. The "Big Store" is in the distance, at the centre is the Willows Hotel, to the right are the Lilelana Pavilion (built by the Thulins in 1918) and the Vanstone Building, built by pioneer David Vanstone in 1929. CRM 10228.

Heriot Bay Inn, Quadra Island, on the occasion of the Bishop's visit, 1916. Hotel owners Mr. and Mrs. Hosea Bull are on the extreme left, Mrs. Scofield and the Right Reverend Bishop Scofield of Victoria are fourth and fifth from the left, Jenny and Mae Miller, maids at the hotel, stand beside post in centre of photo. CRM 4249.

" I lived at Shoal Bay in the '30s. The *Chelohsin* used to leave Vancouver 6:00 p.m. on Monday, and on Tuesday afternoons, everybody came down to the dock to meet the boat.

Our family used to order groceries from Vancouver and they'd come up on the boat. Woodward's was a popular store. David Spencer was the other one. My mother would send her list and her cheque with the boat to Vancouver, and the next week her order would be delivered, and she'd have another order to send. It was a first class service. We never lost anything on the Union boats."

Ross McLeod

When Ross McLeod's family moved to Shoal Bay in the 1930s, the four children brought the number of students to nine, enough to open a school. Ross's mother was the teacher. The school closed when the McLeod family moved away.

Sopa Polla

Serves 6

1	**chicken, cut up**	1

Add chicken pieces to a pot of boiling salted water and simmer for 3 hours. Take out bones, back, neck and skin.

4	**tomatoes, peeled and chopped**	4
1	**hot pepper, minced**	1
2	**onions, minced**	2
3 Tbsp	**chopped fresh cilantro**	45 mL

Add tomatoes, pepper, onion and cilantro to pot. Simmer 1 hour.

3	**avocados**	3
	juice of 1 lime	

Peel and quarter avocados. Just before serving, add avocado and lime juice. Leave long enough to heat, about 5 minutes, and serve.

Gerrie Dinsley

The Union Steamship **Chelohsin** *leaving the old Campbell River wharf. The small vessel at the wharf was Quadra Island's first ferry.* **CRM 5115.**

Curried Cream Consommé

Serves 4
Chill 1 hour

4 oz	**cream cheese**	125 g
10 oz	**canned consommé**	284 mL
1 tsp	**curry powder**	5 mL

Put cream cheese, half the consommé, and the curry powder into blender and blend well. Half fill 4 little pots, cups or cream soup plates and chill 30 minutes or until firm. Slowly pour other half of consommé on top and chill 30 minutes longer or until firm.

edible flowers or leaves

Garnish with flowers or leaves and serve.

Margaret Mae (Forrester) Yorke

The dining room of Painter's Lodge, 1940s. The world-famous Painter's Lodge began with boat rentals and a tent camp for anglers, established by boatbuilder Ned Painter and his wife June in 1922. CRM 11894.

Celia Haig-Brown in the garden
mid-1950s
The Haig-Brown House

VEGETABLES & GRAINS

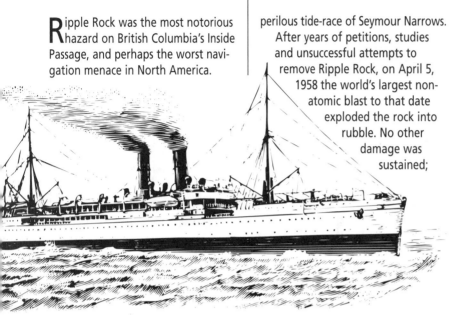

Ripple Rock was the most notorious hazard on British Columbia's Inside Passage, and perhaps the worst navigation menace in North America.

perilous tide-race of Seymour Narrows. After years of petitions, studies and unsuccessful attempts to remove Ripple Rock, on April 5, 1958 the world's largest non-atomic blast to that date exploded the rock into rubble. No other damage was sustained;

"Everybody was optimistic at the time (c. 1914) that the E & N Railway would be extended to Seymour Narrows and a bridge put across there and everybody knew it was politics that kept it from going.

Ripple Rock was supposed to be used as a centre post, a foundation for the centre pier of the bridge. We used to hear that time and time again. It was considered practical by the engineers of that day."

Tom Menzies, a Comox Valley area resident born in 1900

Nine miles north of Campbell River, the twin pinnacles of Ripple Rock wrecked over one hundred ships passing through the

the mammoth undertaking was an engineering triumph.

Yet there were those who had wanted to preserve Ripple Rock.

The explosion of Ripple Rock in Seymour Narrows, April 5, 1958 was a momentous occasion. This classic image of the blast was captured by Vancouver Province photographer R. E. Olsen 6.9 seconds after the detonation. CRM 12148.

Barley & Pine Nut Casserole

Serves 4

½ cup	**pine nuts**	125 mL
1 Tbsp	**butter**	15 mL

Sauté pine nuts in butter and remove from pan.

1 cup	**barley**	250 mL
2 Tbsp	**butter**	30 mL

Rinse and drain barley. Sauté in butter.

1	**medium onion, chopped**	1
½ cup	**minced fresh parsley**	125 mL
¼ cup	**minced chives or green onion**	50 mL
¼ tsp	**salt**	1 mL
¼ tsp	**pepper**	1 mL

Combine pine nuts, barley and remaining ingredients and place in casserole. Preheat oven to 350°F (180°C).

3 cups	**hot chicken or beef broth**	700 mL

Pour hot broth over casserole. Bake uncovered at 350°F (180°C) for 1 hour.

Judy Price Sturgis

" If one woman gets in another's patch, they fight over it. Sometimes they used to pick up sticks and hit each other with them, and their menfolks used to come sometimes, too, and butt in. I have seen fights like this many times when I was a boy. Clover patches are women's property, and it comes down to their daughter. If they have no daughter, the boy gets it, and then when he gets a wife the wife uses it. It is only this way with patches of roots. The berries don't belong to anybody."

Clellan S. Ford, Smoke from Their Fires: The Life of a Kwakiutl Chief

Dot's Potato Casserole

Serves 8

2.2 lbs	**hash browns, frozen**	1 kg
2 cups	**sour cream**	500 mL
20 oz	**condensed cream of mushroom soup** (2 tins)	568 mL
½ cup	**melted butter**	125 mL
	grated onion to taste	
	salt to taste	
2 cups	**grated cheddar cheese**	500 mL

Preheat oven to 350°F (180°C).

Thaw hash browns slightly and mix all ingredients thoroughly. Place in 9x13" (23x33 cm) pan and bake for 1–1½ hours.

Jeanette Taylor

The Pidcock Family's General Store

The Pidcock family settled in Quathiaski Cove on Quadra Island over one hundred years ago and operated a general store there in the early 1900s. Ranchers received credit for produce. The ledger for 1902–06 of Pidcock Bros. & Co., "Dealers in General Merchandise & Manufacturers or Rough & Dressed Lumber," shows that F. C. Yeatman received credit for onions, carrots, turnips, parsnips, deer skins and a log. Among his purchases were a geography, scribblers, spools of thread, yardage, shoes and yarn.

"Pidcock's general store was managed by the eldest brother, William T. The variety of items carried by the store is staggering. Stock included celery compound, perfume, calico, cheviot, Boston pilot, shoe nails, tar soap, bear grease, currycomb, falling wedges, limes, umbrellas, nutmegs, chamber pots, ticking, elastic, chambray, corn cures, pile ointment, sarsaparilla, clover kegs, tinned sardines, oysters and tomatoes."

Ruth (Pidcock) Barnett, *daughter of one of the Pidcock Brothers (George) and granddaughter of original settlers Alice and Reginald Pidcock*

Nettle or Spinach Spanokopita

Serves 8

2 lbs	**nettles or fresh spinach**	900 g

Preheat oven to 350°F (180°C). Steam nettles or spinach until done.

1 cup	**chopped onion**	250 mL
3 Tbsp	**butter**	45 mL
	salt and pepper to taste	
1 tsp	**basil**	5 mL
½ tsp	**oregano**	2 mL
5	**eggs, lightly beaten**	5
2 cups	**crumbled feta cheese**	500 mL
2 Tbsp	**flour**	30 mL
2 cups	**cottage cheese**	500 mL

Sauté onion in butter until soft, seasoning lightly. Combine with remaining ingredients and add nettles or spinach.

	Pastry:	
8 oz	**melted butter**	225 g
1 lb	**filo pastry, defrosted**	450 g
1 Tbsp	**anise or fennel seed** (optional)	15 mL

Spread butter on a 9x13" (23x33 cm) baking pan. Place 1 filo leaf in pan, letting it drape over edges; brush generously with melted butter. Pile 8 leaves, one on top of another, brushing each layer with butter. Spread on half the filling and stack on 8 more layers of buttered filo leaves. Spread remaining filling on top. Fold the excess filo down along the edges. Pile on as many layers of filo and butter as your pan will hold. Butter the topmost leaf and sprinkle with anise or fennel seeds. Bake uncovered in 350°F (180°C) oven for about 45 minutes—until top is golden brown.

Jeanette Taylor

"Of esculent vegetables we found but few; the white or dead nettle, and samphire, were most common; the wild orache, vulgarly called fat-hen, with the vetch. Two or three sorts of wild peas, and the common hedge mustard, were frequently though not always met with, and were considered by us as excellent of their kinds, and served to relish our salt provisions, on which with a very scanty supply of fish, all hands subsisted."

The Voyage of George Vancouver 1791–1795, ed. W. Kaye Lamb

"For though there be no appearance of cultivation amongst them, there are great quantities of alder, gooseberry and currant bushes, whose fruits they may eat in their natural state, as we have seen them eat the leaves of the last, and of the lilies, just as they were plucked from the plant. It must, however, be observed, that one of the conditions which they seem to require, in all food, is, that it should be of the bland or less acrid kind; for they would not eat the leek or garlic, though they brought vast quantities to sell, when they understood we were fond of it. Indeed, they seemed to have no relish for any of our food; and when offered spirituous liquors, they rejected them as something unnatural and disgusting to the palate."

Capt. James Cook,
A Voyage to the Pacific Ocean,
1776–1778

Curry Vegetable Platter

Serves 6–8

1	**large onion, chopped**	1
	minced garlic to taste	
2 Tbsp	**butter**	30 mL
1 Tbsp	**hot curry powder**	15 mL

Sauté onion and garlic in butter until tender. Add curry and cook 2 minutes more.

2½ cups	**vegetable broth or water**	600 mL
1 cup	**uncooked long-grain rice**	250 mL
½ cup	**raisins**	125 mL
1 glass	**chilled wine**	

Add broth and bring to boil. Add rice, cover and simmer 15–30 minutes until water is absorbed. Stir in raisins. Let stand 5 minutes.
Drink wine while waiting.

2	**yams,** cut in 1" (2.5 cm) pieces	2
1 lb	**broccoli,** cut in 1" (2.5 cm) pieces	450 g
1	**cauliflower,** separated into florets	1

Meanwhile steam yams for 5 minutes. Add broccoli and cauliflower. Cover and steam 7–10 minutes more.

2 Tbsp	**melted butter**	30 mL
¼ cup	**sunflower seeds**	50 mL

To serve, spread rice on platter with vegetables arranged on top. Drizzle butter over vegetables. Sprinkle with sunflower seeds and enjoy.

Morgan Ostler

Curried Broccoli & Rice

Serves 8–10

1½ cups	**uncooked long-grain rice**	375 mL

Cook rice, set aside.

3 cups	**fresh broccoli florets,** or 2 pkgs (500 g) frozen	700 mL

Steam broccoli until tender, set aside.

¼ cup	**butter**	50 mL
¾ cup	**chopped onion**	175 mL
¼ cup	**flour**	50 mL

Melt butter in skillet. Sauté onion until soft. Sprinkle on the flour, stir and cook for 2 minutes.

2 cups	**chicken broth**	500 mL
2 cups	**milk**	500 mL
1 Tbsp	**curry powder**	15 mL
	salt and pepper to taste	

Add chicken broth, milk, curry, salt and pepper. Stir to a boil.

	Topping:	
4 Tbsp	**melted butter**	50 mL
1 cup	**bread crumbs**	250 mL

Preheat oven to 350°F (180°C).
Combine melted butter and bread crumbs, sprinkle over casserole. Bake for 30 minutes.

Betty Hoover

"As It Was In The Beginning..."
Rototillers help but gardeners must stoop to conquer.

Hubert Evans,
Mostly Coast People

Mustard Carrots

Serves 4–5

2 lbs	**carrots, sliced**	900 g

Cook carrots until nearly done, and drain. Place in baking dish.

	Sauce:	
¼ cup	**brown sugar**	50 mL
3 Tbsp	**butter**	45 mL
3 Tbsp	**prepared mustard**	45 mL

Melt sugar in butter. Add mustard. Pour sauce on carrots and mix well. Heat in oven until bubbly hot.

chopped fresh parsley

Sprinkle with parsley and serve.

Madge Painter

Mexican Rice

Serves 4

1 cup	**uncooked long-grain rice**	250 mL
¼ cup	**margarine**	50 mL

Sauté rice in margarine until thoroughly coated and slightly browned.

⅓ cup	**chopped onion**	75 mL
1	**garlic clove, minced**	1
2 Tbsp	**chopped green pepper**	30 mL

Add onion, garlic and green pepper, and sauté until onion is tender. Mix well.

1 cup	**tomato sauce**	250 mL

Add tomato sauce and cook until heated.

1½ cups	**boiling chicken stock**	375 mL
½ tsp	**salt**	2 mL
¼ tsp	**white pepper**	1 mL

Add chicken stock, salt and pepper. Cover tightly and cook over low heat for 20 minutes. This is an excellent accompaniment for most kinds of enchiladas, burritos and chilies rellenos.

Bill Harrison

Indian Rice

The bulb of the Chocolate Lily (*Fritillaria camschatcensis*) commonly called Indian rice, resembles a cluster of cooked rice grains. The plant is a good source of starch and sugar and since prehistoric times it has been dug in the fall and powdered for winter use. David Nelson, botanist on the *Resolution*, visited "Kamtschatka" in 1778 (shortly before Captain Cook's murder in 1779) and found the natives eating the bulbs of a plant with flowers of "exceeding dark red colour," now thought to be the present species.

Risotto alla Parmigiana

Serves 6–8

½ cup	**butter, softened**	125 mL
½ cup	**chopped onion**	125 mL
	freshly ground pepper to taste	
3–4 Tbsp	**white wine**	45–50 mL

Melt half the butter and add onions, frying them gently until soft. Add pepper to taste. Add wine and boil until wine evaporates.

2 cups	**uncooked rice, Italian or pearl**	500 mL
4½ cups	**beef stock**	1025 mL

Add wine mixture to rice and cook, stirring, for 2–3 minutes as rice absorbs mixture. Cook gently 20–25 minutes, stirring frequently and gradually adding hot beef stock to moisten rice. When rice is tender, remove from heat.

1 cup	**grated parmesan cheese**	250 mL

Add remaining butter and parmesan. Fold in gently and serve.

Katia Panziera

Jay's Tabouli

Serves 4–6

1 cup	**bulgur**	250 mL
1 cup	**warm water**	250 mL

Soak bulgur in water 2 hours or until soft. Drain excess water if any.

1 cup	**chopped cucumber**	250 mL
2–3	**tomatoes, chopped**	2–3
1 cup	**chopped fresh parsley**	250 mL
½ cup	**chopped red onion**	125 mL
¼ cup	**chopped fresh mint**	50 mL

Add cucumber, tomato, parsley, onion and mint to bulgur.

	Dressing:	
⅓ cup	**oil**	75 mL
⅓ cup	**fresh lemon juice**	75 mL
1	**garlic clove, pressed**	1

Combine all dressing ingredients. Toss bulgur mixture with dressing, chill and serve. Tabouli keeps well in the fridge for 2–3 days if you do not add the vegetables and mint until just before serving.

Jay Stewart

Forbes Landing on Campbell Lake, 1950. CRM 1429.

Resting in the undercut.
Kenneth Houghton-Brown at Blind Channel, BC
c. 1935
CRM 7269

PASTA

Mrs. Suduth of California, winner of a Bronze Button, with her 32½-pound tyee, September 1939. Painter's Lodge is in the background. CRM 18518.

Seafood Lasagna

Serves 8

8	lasagna noodles	8

Cook lasagna according to directions and place half of them in a 9x13" (23x33 cm) pan.

1 cup	chopped onion	250 mL
2 Tbsp	butter	30 mL
8 oz	cream cheese, softened	225 g
1½ cups	cottage cheese	375 mL
1	egg, beaten	1
2 tsp	basil	10 mL
½ tsp	salt	2 mL
	pepper to taste	

Sauté onion in butter. Mix in cream cheese, cottage cheese, egg, basil, salt and pepper. Spread half of this mixture over noodles.

20 oz	condensed cream of mushroom soup (2 tins)	568 mL
⅓ cup	milk	75 mL
⅓ cup	dry white wine or vermouth	75 mL
4¼ oz	crab meat, canned or fresh cooked	120 g
1 lb	shrimp, shelled, deveined and cooked	450 g

In a separate bowl, combine soup, milk and wine. Stir in crab and shrimp. Spoon half of this mixture over cheese layer. Repeat all layers, ending with seafood layer. Preheat oven to 350°F (180°C).

¼ cup	grated parmesan cheese	50 mL

Sprinkle with parmesan cheese. Bake uncovered for 45 minutes.

½ cup	grated sharp cheddar cheese	125 mL

Top lasagna with cheddar cheese and brown under broiler. Let stand 15 minutes to set before serving.

Hope Ross

Amalia's Lasagna

Serves 10

8 oz	**lasagna noodles**	225 g

Cook noodles according to package directions. (I use 2 packages fresh lasagna and I don't precook it.)

	Meat Sauce:	
2 Tbsp	**oil**	30 mL
2 Tbsp	**butter**	30 mL
2	**onions, minced**	2
1 lb	**lean ground beef**	450 g
8 oz	**lean ground pork**	225 g
7	**garlic cloves, crushed**	7
1½ tsp	**salt**	7 mL
¼ tsp	**pepper**	1 mL
½ tsp	**oregano**	2 mL
½ tsp	**basil**	2 mL
3 Tbsp	**chopped fresh parsley**	5 mL
1 cup	**tomato sauce**	250 mL
1 cup	**tomato paste**	250 mL
2 cups	**water**	500 mL

Heat oil and butter and sauté onion until golden brown. Add beef and pork and cook for 10–15 minutes, stirring to break up the meat. Mix in remaining ingredients and simmer 1–2½ hours. When ready to assemble, make White Sauce.

	White Sauce:	
3 Tbsp	**butter**	45 mL
6 Tbsp	**flour**	90 mL
2 cups	**milk**	500 mL
1 cup	**light cream**	250 mL
1 tsp	**salt**	5 mL
¼ tsp	**nutmeg**	1 mL

Melt butter, add flour and stir. Add milk and cream, bring to a boil and turn down heat. Add salt and nutmeg, stirring constantly.

3 cups	**white sauce or**	700 mL
1 lb	**cottage cheese**	450 g
½ cup	**grated parmesan cheese**	125 mL
1 lb	**mozzarella cheese, grated**	450 g

Preheat oven to 375°F (190°C).

Spread about 1 cup (250 mL) meat sauce on the bottom of a 9x13" (23x33 cm) pan. Layer on a third of the pasta sheets. Spread with meat sauce, then a layer of white sauce or cottage cheese, then about 2 Tbsp (30 mL) parmesan and a generous layer of grated mozzarella. Repeat twice. Bake for 30 minutes, uncovered. Let cool 10–15 minutes to set before serving.

Amalia Tancon

Wearing what appears to be their Sunday best this couple brings a recently slaughtered pig to a community picnic. Early settlers had few opportunities for social interaction but made the most of them when occasions arose.

Pasta & Filetto Sauce

Serves 6

3 cups	**fresh pasta**	700 mL

Cook pasta of your choice *al dente*.

	Filetto Sauce:	
2 Tbsp	**oil**	30 mL
2	**garlic cloves, minced**	2
2	**large onions, minced**	2
1 tsp	**chopped fresh oregano, or** ½ tsp (2 mL) **dried oregano**	5 mL
2 Tbsp	**chopped fresh basil, or** 2 tsp (10 mL) **dried**	30 mL
¼ tsp	**red pepper flakes**	1 mL
¾ tsp	**salt**	3 mL
	pepper to taste	

Heat oil and sauté garlic for a minute or two. Add onions and sauté until tender. Add remaining herbs and spices.

1½ lbs	**fresh plum tomatoes, peeled, seeded and chopped, or** 28 oz (798 mL) **canned plum tomatoes, chopped**	675 g
½ tsp	**sugar**	2 mL

Add tomatoes and sugar and simmer uncovered for 30 minutes, stirring occasionally.

	Pasta Sauce:	
1 Tbsp	**butter**	15 mL
2 Tbsp	**olive oil**	30 mL
6	**mushrooms, sliced**	6
2	**garlic cloves, minced**	2
8	**chicken livers, coarsely chopped**	8

Heat butter and oil and sauté mushrooms for 2 minutes. Remove mushrooms from pan and sauté garlic for 1 minute. Add livers and cook until light brown. Add cooked mushrooms.

1 lb	ground sirloin	450 g
	salt and pepper to taste	
1	recipe Filetto Sauce (above)	1
½ cup	whipping cream	125 mL

In another skillet, cook sirloin, salt and pepper for 6 minutes. Add mushroom mixture and Filetto Sauce and simmer for 5 minutes. Stir in cream. When sauce is hot, toss half of it with hot cooked pasta.

1 cup	grated parmesan cheese	250 mL
3 Tbsp	butter	45 mL

Add half of the parmesan cheese and toss again. Add butter and toss again. Place remaining sauce on top and sprinkle with the rest of the parmesan.

Brenda Hancock

Quadra Island settlers gather for a picnic at Rebecca Spit in 1902. CRM 4363.

Salmon Cannelloni with Creamy Lemon Sauce

Serves 6–7

	Filling:	
7½ oz	**canned salmon, drained and flaked**	213 g
½ cup	**sour cream**	125 mL
2	**green onions, chopped**	2
½ tsp	**grated lemon rind**	2 mL
¼ tsp	**salt**	1 mL

Combine salmon, sour cream, onions, lemon rind and salt.

12–14	**oven-ready cannelloni**	12–14

Spoon filling into cannelloni. Set aside.

	Sauce:	
3 Tbsp	**butter or margarine**	45 mL
3 Tbsp	**flour**	45 mL
2½ cups	**milk**	600 mL
½ tsp	**dried dill**	2 mL
½ tsp	**salt**	2 mL
1 cup	**shredded swiss cheese**	250 mL
2 Tbsp	**lemon juice**	30 mL

In saucepan, melt butter and stir in flour. Add milk, dill, salt and half the cheese. Cook and stir until bubbling and smooth. Remove from heat. Stir in lemon juice.

Preheat oven to 350°F (180°C). Pour a thin layer of sauce on bottom of greased 9x13" (23x33 cm) baking dish. Place cannelloni in a single layer and cover with remaining sauce and cheese. Cover dish and bake for 35–40 minutes.

¼ cup	**pine nuts** (optional)	50 mL

If desired, sprinkle with pine nuts and put under broiler until slightly browned.

Gloria Cameron

Pesto Linguine

Serves 4

1 lb	**linguine**	450 g

Cook linguine *al dente*.

	Sauce:	
1 cup	**chopped fresh basil**	250 mL
4	**fresh parsley sprigs, minced**	4
2	**fresh marjoram sprigs**	2
½ cup	**pine nuts**	125 mL
1	**garlic clove, minced**	1
⅓ cup	**grated parmesan cheese**	75 mL
⅓ cup	**grated romano cheese**	75 mL
¼ cup	**olive oil**	50 mL
2 Tbsp	**butter**	30 mL
½ tsp	**salt**	2 mL

Combine next 10 ingredients in a saucepan.

½ cup	**chicken stock**	125 mL

Add stock and simmer on medium heat for 10 minutes. Toss sauce with hot cooked linguine.

½ cup	**grated parmesan cheese**	125 mL

Sprinkle with parmesan cheese and serve.

Estelle Inman

❞ I came to Campbell River in 1925. One summer I was asked to keep house for Mr. Berg in his big log house on Campbell Lake—the building that later turned out to be the first Strathcona Lodge. It was brand new then. Mr. Berg was a rich American who used to fly up every summer.

Mr. Anderson, the Swedish caretaker, always planted a garden and we always had lots of vegetables. I used wild onions to flavour my stews. I would get them from the woods around the lodge.

The only way we could get out was to go across the lake. At that time Elk River Timber Company had a boat running up the lake and Cecil Haycock would bring in the mail and supplies for us.

Behind that lodge there was a great big cellar dug in the side of the hill and it was full of all kinds of wines. Mr. Berg's millionaire friends would fly in and bring all kinds of wines and liquors and they would store it in this cellar. I often wondered what happened to this cellar because Mr. Berg died the summer after I was there."

Gwen Telosky, *CRM aural history*

The Long Journey of the Potato

As early as the fifteenth century, Spanish explorers discovered the potato in South America. They took it back to Europe where it was enthusiastically cultivated, and travellers introduced it to Africa, India, Malaysia, China and Japan. When the British settled in BC and began to trade with the local aboriginal people, they were quite surprised to find potatoes among the trading commodities of the Haida. Marius Barbeau suggested the potato found its way back to North America by being carried from Japan and the East Indies to islands in the Pacific Ocean, where the Haida encountered it in their travels.

Native village at Yan, Queen Charlotte Islands. BCARS 41054.

Perogies

Makes about 50 perogies

	Dough:	
2 cups	**flour**	500 mL
¼ cup	**oil**	50 mL
dash	**salt**	dash
½–¾ cup	**warm water**	125–175 mL

Blend dough ingredients until smooth. Roll dough thin and cut circles with a large round cookie cutter or tin can with ends cut out.

	Filling:	
2 cups	**dry cottage cheese**	500 mL
2	**eggs**	2
½ tsp	**salt**	2 mL

Mix all filling ingredients together. Place a spoonful of filling in the centre of a dough circle, fold over and seal (dip your finger in water, dampen the edges and then pinch edges together).

Heat a large pot of salted water to a full rolling boil. Drop in perogies a few at a time. Boil for about 10 minutes, drain in a colander and rinse with clear water. Set aside as you cook them.

8 oz	**bacon, chopped**	225 g
1	**onion, diced**	1

Sauté bacon and onion in frying pan. Place perogies in the pan with bacon and onion one layer at a time. Fry until hot, turning once. Continue until all perogies are reheated.

	sour cream to taste	

Serve perogies with the cooked bacon and onion, and sour cream.

Eileen Odowichuk

A day's catch.
Outside the Willows Hotel, Campbell River, BC, 1950
CRM 1381

FISH & SEAFOOD

"When the run of Spring or Tyee Salmon is on one is able to capture large fish, sometimes of fifty and sixty pounds. One uses a short trolling rod, one hundred and fifty or two hundred yards of line on a strong reel, three ounce lead, and a silver or copper spoon some three and half inches long, to which is attached a single hook made in the Indian pattern. The tide runs very strong at the mouth of the [Campbell] river, the ebb tide flowing north ..."

from Francis Barrow's journal

A very large salmon photographed at the Goose Bay Cannery, Rivers Inlet on August 1, 1939. This tyee weighed in at 105 lbs., was 54 inches long and 18 inches wide.

The Five Species of Salmon

Chinook/Spring/King/Tyee
[*Oncorhynchus tshawytscha*]: The largest of the salmon species with a high oil content. Colouring from red to ivory. Very flavourful.

Coho/Silver [*Oncorhynchus kisutch*]: A
drier fish with less oil content and a red flesh. Full-flavoured.

Chum/Dog Salmon [*Oncorhynchus keta*]: Pink to medium red flesh with
a high oil content. Excellent for smoking. Called keta when canned. Mild flavour.

Sockeye [*Oncorhynchus nerka*]: A
deep red flesh and high oil content. Rich flavour. Sockeye is derived from the Native word *Sau-kai*, meaning chief.

Pink/Humpy [*Oncorhynchus gorbuscha*]: The smallest of the
salmon species. Pink coloured with a delicate texture. Very tasty.

Buying and Cooking Fish
British Columbia salmon is world renowned for taste, freshness and quality. The paramount rule for cooking all fish is to AVOID OVERCOOKING. Always measure fish at its thickest part for doneness; for each inch of thickness cook 10 minutes at high heat. Add 5 minutes per inch if wrapped in foil or heavily sauced. When the fish is done, the flesh is opaque and flakes readily. To eat raw fish (e.g. sushi), it must first be frozen for 7 days at -10°F (-23°C), then thawed and sliced.

Follow these simple steps to test fish for freshness:
• The eyes should be clear, not dull and milky
• Flesh should be firm and elastic and not leave an impression when gently pressed.
• There should be no fishy smell.
• There should be little or no scale loss.
• There should not be any blood showing inside the flesh.
• Flesh should not be mushy or have any gaping.

Barbecued Salmon Marinade

Makes enough for 1 salmon
Marinate 8 hours

1	whole salmon	1

Scale and fillet salmon, cut it into serving pieces.

	Marinade:	
⅓ cup	oil	75 mL
1	garlic clove, pressed	
3 Tbsp	soy sauce	45 mL
½ cup	rye whiskey	125 mL
2 Tbsp	sugar	30 mL
	salt and pepper to taste	
½	bottle beer	½

Combine marinade ingredients and marinate fish for 8 hours. Start with skin side up and turn occasionally. Barbecue for a delicious dinner.

Madge Painter

"More people smoke dog salmon than anything else. At Kingcome, they used to go way up the river, to smoke their fish. The fish are better quality for the Indian style of smoking than they are down at the mouth. At the mouth, they are still pretty oily, pretty fat. Oily fish gets rancid."

Jim Henderson,
CRM aural history

"I started out when we were married going fishing with my husband. In the fall of '32 and the summer of '33, we were getting two cents each for a dog salmon. Friends in Ocean Falls would send us little wooden kegs and ask for a keg of salted dog salmon bellies for the winter. So we'd just cut the bellies out and throw away the rest."

Flora Brendeland,
CRM aural history
Born in 1912, Flora Brendeland lived in many locations along the BC coast.

Smoked Salmon

Barbecued Salmon, Kwakwaka'wakw Style

In this traditional method of barbecuing, the salmon is slow-cooked near a smouldering fire, giving it a moist, delicious, smoky taste and texture.

For each salmon, the cook uses a cedar stick about 4' (10 cm) long and 1–2" (3–5 cm) in diameter, split about three-fourths of the way down the middle. She slits the fresh salmon down the back, cleans it and removes the back-bone. Then she slits it almost all the way through and flattens it. At this point she might rub the fish with onion, lemon juice, brown sugar, vinegar or other condi-ments, or the fish can be cooked just as it is.

She slides the flattened fish down the split in the stick, neck end at the bottom. With the skin side down, she inserts a few small-er cedar sticks horizontally between the stick and the fish to hold it flat. Then she weaves in vertical sticks as necessary and ties the top ends of the split stick together.

To cook the fish, she places it so that it leans toward a smouldering wood fire, either by sharpening the bottom of the stick and push-ing it in the ground, or by leaning the fish against a pole or other support. A 5–10 lb (3–4.5 kg) salmon takes about an hour. The cook watches the fish carefully and keeps the fire smouldering.

Clams, oysters and mussels can be cooked the same way.

Marinate 5 hours; dry overnight

1	**whole salmon**	1

Scale and fillet salmon. Leave skin on. Cut crosswise into chunks.

	Brine:	
½ cup	**brown sugar**	125 mL
½ cup	**pickling salt**	125 mL
1 cup	**water**	250 mL
½ cup	**pickling spice**	125 mL

Mix all brine ingredients together and marinate salmon pieces for 5 hours. Put on racks to drain, skin side down. Dry overnight until surface feels sticky. Follow directions for smoking in a Little Chief smoker.

Madge Painter

Native style barbecued salmon at Museum Day, Campbell River, 1983. CRM 15783.

Smoked Salmon

"As soon as we got there, we would take down the long sticks (ga'yu) on which the salmon would be hung for smoking. We would scrub these—there were lots of them, because there were two layers of them hung up.

The house would then be swept out, using branches of trees tied to the end of a pole. When everything was clean and ready, then they would go out to spear, they did not often hook salmon there. The best dried fish was made from fish that was speared.

Over two hundred at a time would be caught by one man. It was sometimes very cold and the fish would be frozen.

When the catch was brought up onto the beach, Gana and her mother-in-law, Ga'aaxsta'las, would begin to cut them. When they were finished, I would carry them up from the beach in buckets. By evening, that would be finished, we would eat supper, then they would begin to fillet the fish. It would take all night. When that was finished, the fillets would be hung up. After these were all hung up, another catch would be brought in,

"Our camp at the mouth of the Campbell River ... The salmon on the right weighed fifty-four pounds, that on the left some five pounds less." Francis J. Barrow, c. 1898. CRM 11490.

over two hundred again. These would be for her brother.

While these were being cleaned and filleted, my job was to turn those which were already hung up. They would have to be turned several times each day. They were said to be 'lying on their backs' on a log. The next day, they were lying face down on a log. Every day, over two hundred fish were brought in, cleaned, filleted and hung up to dry. Those prepared the first day were hung closest to the ceiling of the house, those prepared the following days were hung on lower levels."

U'Mista Cultural Society, Alert Bay, BC

Irene's Pickled Salmon

Makes 6 qts (6 L)

Salt for 4 days

1	20-lb (9 kg) **whole salmon**	1
	pickling salt	

Split salmon, remove backbone and skin. Cut into pieces about 4" (10 cm) long, and layer pieces in a glass or ceramic bowl, sprinkling each layer with pickling salt. Make sure salmon is completely covered with salt and leave it in the refrigerator for at least 4 days.

Wash salt off and slice fish thinly. Soak fish slices in cold water until there is no salty taste. I usually change the water four or five times.

Brine:		
1 cup	**sugar**	250 mL
2 cups	**vinegar**	500 mL
6–8 cups	**water**	1.5–2 L

Make a thin brine of sugar, vinegar and water. Soak fish in this for about an hour. This will remove any fishy taste. Drain.

Pickling Solution:		
2 cups	**white sugar**	500 mL
3 cups	**ketchup**	750 mL
3	**large onions, chopped**	
½ cup	**chopped sweet pickle**	125 mL
12	**bay leaves**	12
¼ cup	**allspice**	50 mL
½ cup	**whole dried chili peppers**	125 mL
4 cups	**white vinegar**	900 mL

Mix all pickling ingredients together. Combine pickling solution with fish pieces in clean jars or plastic containers and keep in fridge.

Irene Ross

"The smokehouses at U'dzo'la's were the biggest I ever saw. People lived in them. Anitsala had a big house, big enough for four families, with four levels of hanging racks. The fires were carefully tended, so that they did not burn too hot. Maybe six or seven hundred fish hanging at one time. There was a big flat piece of metal put over the fire, so the smoke would go up around the edges, not go straight up the smoke hole."

Leonard Ham, *Preliminary Survey of Nimpkish Heritage Sites, October 1980; U'mista oral history tapes*

Richard's Pickled Salmon

Makes 1 whole salmon

1	whole salmon	1
	oil	
	salt and pepper to taste	

Fillet and skin salmon. Cut into bite-sized chunks. Fry chunks in oil and season with salt and pepper. Drain well on paper towels.

Brine:
vinegar
honey
water
fresh sliced ginger root to taste

Combine all brine ingredients. Use equal parts of vinegar, honey and water, and add ginger to taste. Make enough brine to cover the fish.

sliced onions to taste

Add lots of raw onions to the cooked fish. Pour the brine over to cover. Serve cold.

Richard Krentz

" In 1926, in Area 12 [Queen Charlotte Strait] there might have been a dozen boats fishing. But not long after that I saw two hundred and fifty boats tied up in Alert Bay in one weekend. They've got so much gear out now.

The Yugoslav fishermen started the blind set business and we used to laugh at them making blind sets. We always ran around looking for a bunch of fish to set on, looked for lots of jumpers. They just kept on plugging away and now they are all blind setting. The only time you make a set now is if you can find room to put your net in the water."

Jim Henderson,
CRM aural history

A gathering on the beach to weigh fish, 1930s. Mrs. Weeks and her salmon are at centre.
CRM 6018.

"Old-timers will remember the shacks along the beach between Cape Mudge and Francisco Point where Indians and Whites built their separate villages from beach wood. There was another cluster of about twenty shacks at Poverty Point (now called April Point). Most of the people who fished here were down on their luck. Many were doctors, lawyers—professional people. They managed to earn some money fishing for the Cannery using a minimum of gear and a canoe or a rowboat, a bit of line attached to a stick, a spoon and a hook.

The first cannery at Quathiaski Cove was opened by the Pidcock brothers in 1904. It burned, was rebuilt, and in 1912 was transferred to the Quathiaski Canning Company Ltd., with W. E. Anderson as manager and principal owner. The complex included a store, net loft and coal shed. The cannery owned the rights to the salmon in Johnstone Strait between Cape Mudge and Kelsey Bay. To harvest their fish, cannery workers built a commercial fish trap at Plumper Bay, an arrangement of piles which funnelled the fish into an enclosure where they could be brailed into a packer. Anderson built a cannery at Blind Channel also, in order to qualify for the rights to a second section of the Strait."

Bill Hall, *CRM aural history*
The Hall family pre-empted land on Quadra Island in 1902 and Bill Hall was born there in 1904. His working life included logging, prospecting, mining, towboating, commercial fishing and operating the first Quadra Island ferry.

Poached Salmon in Wine

Serves 6

2 lbs	**salmon fillets**	900 g
½ tsp	**salt**	2 mL
¼ tsp	**pepper**	1 mL
	thinly sliced green pepper	

Arrange fish in shallow pan, sprinkle with salt and pepper and cover with green pepper.

2 Tbsp	**Worcestershire sauce**	30 mL
½ cup	**sauterne wine**	125 mL

Sprinkle with Worcestershire and wine. Marinate 30 minutes (15 minutes per side).

2 Tbsp	**butter**	30 mL
1	**lemon, sliced**	1
1	**onion, sliced**	1
¼ cup	**chopped fresh parsley**	50 mL

Preheat oven to 350°F (180°C). Dot salmon with butter. Place lemon and onion slices on top and sprinkle on the parsley. Bake for 20–30 minutes. To check doneness, insert fork in thickest part of fish. It should be moist and still pinkish.

Gerrie Dinsley

Maud Island Salmon

Serves 8

1	**whole salmon**	1
	sliced onions	
	sliced lemons	
	sliced oranges	
	bacon strips	
	salt and pepper to taste	
	garlic powder to taste	
	soy sauce (optional)	

Clean salmon, cut in half lengthwise and remove backbone. Do not fillet. On half the salmon, place a layer of sliced onions, lemons, oranges and top with bacon and seasonings. Cover with top half of salmon and lay more bacon on top. Wrap in foil and barbecue about 20 minutes on each side.

Win Mayse

Fishing boat on the Inside Passage.
CRM 8250.

"Real Springs spawn in April and into June. The Tyee, he was separate. The white man, he calls them all Chinook now. The Tyee, he's about ninety percent red. The other fellow, he's just the opposite. He's pretty well all white. Troll-caught fish were always considered a little better. They were gutted right away and put in ice. In the '20s, ice had to be hauled from Vancouver. The next place was up north at Butedale. They made ice there.

The Quathiaski Cannery had their own people here at Cape Mudge and Campbell River but the Rivers Inlet crew used to come up from Vancouver, Squamish and Duncan. They'd all go to Vancouver and get on the Union Steamship. I've seen that old *Camosun* come up—I'd be waiting by the gang. I've seen at least twelve hundred people aboard her, cannery workers, you know. Just crawling over one another. Plumb full of people. Some drunk. It used to be quite a 'do' when the Rivers Inlet crew would come up. In the '20s, there were about thirty canneries in Rivers [Inlet]. For five to six weeks there was lots of excitement.

I was bossman for Margaret Bay. My job was to line up fishermen and cannery workers. The women were cannery fillers. Some bossmen for the sockeye were bossmen of the hop fields, too. They'd move their crew down to the Fraser Valley hop fields after fishing was over. Some used to work in the canneries on the Fraser after Rivers Inlet."

Jim Henderson,
CRM aural history

A favourite traditional delicacy among Native people of the West Coast was "Indian cheese," made from salmon eggs. The cook would clean a deer stomach, then put in chum or coho eggs and set it aside. Each day she would knead the stomach, until eventually a "cheese" formed.

Winter Harbour Salmon

Serves 4–6

2 lbs	spring salmon fillet	900 g
	salt and pepper to taste	

Cut salmon into pieces about 2x2" (5x5 cm) and season to taste. Partially frozen fish works best to retain the moisture while cooking.

	Batter:	
½ cup	cornstarch	150 mL
1 tsp	vinegar	5 mL
⅓ cup	flour	75 mL
1 tsp	baking powder	5 mL
1¼ cups	beer or water	300 mL

Combine all batter ingredients to make a medium thick batter. Dip fish in batter and deep fry about 3–4 minutes until golden.

Gerrie Dinsley

The Haida village of Ninstints, Queen Charlotte Islands, 1898. BCARS HP96392.

Baked Salmon Eggs

salmon eggs, fresh or frozen

Lay eggs, still in film, on cookie sheet.

melted butter or margarine

salt and pepper to taste

Preheat oven to 350°F (180°C).

Roll eggs in melted butter, sprinkle with salt and pepper. Bake for 15–20 minutes or until eggs are brown all over.

Break off a section of the baked eggs and eat. They will be nice and chewy.

Amy Quatell (Mucksun)

"This Fish [salmon] we observed was reserved for occasions of Great festivity, and though apparently in great abundance, in every hut in the Village, yet it was with much reluctance that they were prevailed on to sell one of them, and a Sea Otter skin was not purchased at a dearer rate than a Salmon."

James Strange's Journal and Narrative of the Commercial Expedition from Bombay to the Northwest Coast of America, A. V. Ayyar et al

Salmon Sukiyaki

Processing the salmon harvest has been going on for hundreds of years. Natives dried it for their own use and for trading. Early settlers salted it for export.

In 1917 there were ninety-four canneries along the coast. Today there are only a handful.

"The cannery at Blind Channel was closed but the Japanese used the building as a saltery in the fall. The seine boats flocked in there. The thousands and thousands of salmon were stacked up like cordwood. They'd box them and send them to Japan."

Walter Sovde, a longtime logger who has lived on the Coast all his life, CRM aural history

Serves 4

1 lb	**sockeye or spring salmon fillets**	450 g

Cut the fish on an angle in slices ¼" (.5 cm) thick. Set aside.

8 cups	**sliced vegetables**	1800 mL

Use at least four types of vegetables, e.g. onions, green beans, asparagus, carrots, broccoli, mushrooms, zucchini, red pepper.

	Sauce:	
½ cup	**soy sauce**	125 mL
3 Tbsp	**white sugar**	45 mL
¼ cup	**saki or white wine**	50 mL

Mix all sauce ingredients together. If it is too salty for your taste, add a little water.

3 cups	**hot cooked rice**	700 mL

In a large electric frying pan at the table, heat enough sauce to cover the bottom. Add a few of each vegetable, the ones which need most cooking first. Add salmon slices last—they need very little cooking. Serve over bowls of rice and cook another pan full for seconds.

	bean thread noodles (optional)	

Cut noodles into bite-sized pieces and cook 1 minute in boiling water, then refresh in cold water. Sauté with vegetables.

Ross Kondo

Japanese Canadians played a pioneering role in BC lumber camps as well as in the fishing industry. In 1930, these two millhands enlivened their off-hours at Englewood by practising kendo.

Salmon Crunch Pie

Makes one 10" (25 cm) pie

	Filling:	
15 oz	**canned salmon**	426 mL
1 cup	**sour cream**	250 mL
½ cup	**shredded sharp cheddar cheese**	125 mL
3	**eggs, beaten**	3
¼ cup	**mayonnaise**	50 mL
1 Tbsp	**grated onion**	15 mL
¼ tsp	**dill**	1 mL
drop	**Tabasco sauce**	drop

Mix all filling ingredients together and set aside.

	Crust:	
1½ cups	**whole wheat flour**	375 mL
1 cup	**shredded sharp cheddar cheese**	250 mL
½ tsp	**salt**	2 mL
½ tsp	**paprika**	2 mL
½ cup	**butter**	125 mL
⅓ cup	**finely chopped almonds**	75 mL

Mix flour, cheese, salt and paprika together. Cut in butter, making crumbs.
Add almonds and mix.

Preheat oven to 400°F (200°C). Reserve 1 cup (250 mL) of crust mixture
for top and press remaining onto bottom and sides of a 10" (25 cm) pie plate.
Fill with salmon mixture and cover with remaining crumb mixture. Bake for
45 minutes.

Shara Berger

"We worked piece work in the Cannery at Quathiaski Cove. The Chinese would bring bins of fish cut in slices to the packing tables where we filled half flat or one-pound cans. For the half flats, we got four cents for a tray of forty-eight cans and for the tall one-pounds, it was six cents for a tray of twenty-four. When the Cannery whistle blew, we knew the fish boats were in, both day or night, and dropped everything and headed for work. One day I remember Dad and I were papering the ceiling and I had to leave him alone with the bucket of paste and the sticky mess."

Eve (Willson) Eade,
from memoirs at CRM Archives

At the peak of its activity in the 1940s, Rivers Inlet boasted over twenty major salmon canneries.

"The eulachon is a small delicate member of the smelt family. The word 'eulachon' is derived from Chinook, a trade language constructed out of elements of North Coast First Nations languages, English and French. Many spelling variations can be found; eulachon, eulachan, oolachons, oolichan, oolican, ooligan, oulachon, oulachen, hooligan, ulichan, and hollikan.

To many First Nations people, the eulachon are known as 'salvation' or 'saviour' fish because they were the first fish to arrive at the end of winter when most of the stored food supplies were depleted. Eulachons are also known as 'candlefish' or 'lamp-fish' because it is reported that First Nations people and early white settlers would burn the dried oily fish like candles.

Eulachon have been important to North Coast First Nations for thousands of years. Historically, large tribal populations congregated at major fishing sites to fish, process and trade for eulachon and eulachon oil. People travelled by canoe or overland on arduous, well-established trading or 'grease' trails. Although fewer people harvest and utilize the fish today, they remain significant in First Nations diets. They are eaten fresh, smoked, salted or rendered into 'grease'.

Nutritional analyses of eulachon grease in 1981 showed that it is a nutrient-rich food fat, superior to other common fats in providing Vitamin A, E and K. Mainly used to accent the flavour of other foods, especially dried salmon, halibut, seaweed and berries, the 'grease' also has reported medicinal properties."

Westcoast Fisherman, June 1993
Eulachon oil is still made in Knight Inlet each year and still prized by the Kwakwaka'wakw. It is often served at potlatch feasts as a dip or sauce. 'Grease' now sells for one hundred dollars per gallon or more.

Drying eulachons on the Nass River, northern British Columbia. BCARS.

Eulachons

eulachons
flour
pepper to taste

Gut eulachons and roll in peppered flour.

beaten egg
cracker crumbs

Dip in beaten egg and roll in fine cracker crumbs.

cooking oil for deep frying

Deep-fry eulachons until golden brown.

Betty Schmidt

"Every year, early in the spring, the oolichan swam to the rivers to spawn and we would fish them in Kingcome Inlet. The fish were so thick that you couldn't see the bottom of the river, and it was easy to scoop them out of the water ... We ate fresh oolichan until we couldn't eat any more, but with a washtub full it didn't make much of a dent. Preserving food in those days often presented a challenge. Mother used jars and put up berries, salmon, deer meat and deer stew. Many people had a smokehouse, and smoked salmon, cod, halibut, deer and oolichan. We didn't do that, but we always had a stone crock containing oolichan in brine. Mom would take out enough for a feed and give them a good rinse, then put them to soak overnight. The next morning she would change the water, and that night she dried them off, dredged them in flour, and fried them in bacon fat. We would have a feed fit for a king. Mmmm!"

Florence Tickner,
Fish Hooks & Caulk Boots

Rivers Inlet Cannery gearing up for the salmon season, 1920s. VMM.

"In August the Campbell [River] is no big stream for the ascent of thirty and forty-pounders; I have seen them many times, flashing their broad red sides right out in the sunlight to work up over the bar in the Island Pool, rolling out in the fast run under the north bank, even jumping high in the air and crashing back on their bellies within three or four feet of my trout rod. All these fish were moving upstream, showing their progress plainly by successive jumps or rolls or the wave of their passing on shallows."

Roderick Haig-Brown,
A River Never Sleeps

Mary Harry, Nora Wilson, Eva Wilson, Louise Henshall at Redonda Bay Cannery Wharf, 1942. All but Louise are from Churchhouse. CRM 8386.

Fish Mulligan Stew

Serves 6–8

3–4	**potatoes, chopped**	3–4
1	**onion, chopped**	1
	salt and pepper to taste	
4 cups	**uncooked pink salmon pieces**	900 mL

Boil potatoes and onions in enough water so vegetables are covered. Add salt and pepper. When vegetables are almost soft, add fish pieces and simmer 5–10 minutes until fish is done.

	ƛ'ina (eulachon grease) (optional)

Add eulachon grease to taste at this point, or later to individual servings (about 1 Tbsp/15 mL per serving).

Eleanor Cliffe

Halibut Caper Bake

Serves 2

1 lb	**halibut fillets**	450 g
	salt to taste	
	pepper to taste	
	flour	

Sprinkle both sides of fillets with salt, pepper and flour.

⅓ cup	**butter**	75 mL

Sauté fish in butter until brown. Reduce heat and cook for about 5 minutes, remove from heat and keep warm.

	Sauce:	
⅓ cup	**dry white wine**	75 mL
	juice of 1 lemon	
½ cup	**whipping cream**	125 mL
2 Tbsp	**capers, drained**	30 mL
1 Tbsp	**chopped fresh parsley**	15 mL
½ tsp	**chopped fresh basil**	2 mL
	salt and pepper to taste	

Deglaze the skillet with wine. Add lemon juice, mix well and simmer for 3 minutes. Add cream and stir until blended. Simmer until volume is reduced by one-half. Add remaining sauce ingredients and stir until well blended.

chopped fresh parsley

Coat fillets with sauce, garnish with parsley and serve.

Estelle Inman

" In the early days of hand trolling all a fisherman had was a canoe or rowboat, a home-made spoon and herring rake, a hook and a length of cotton line. For many, fishing was only a means of earning enough cash to buy what one couldn't raise, catch, hunt or trade. It brought money for tools, clothing and the like. You didn't make a heck of a lot, but then it went a lot further than it does now, you know. I mean, you never got rich at it, but you got enough to put food on the table … you had your own vegetables and fruit, and all you needed was sugar and flour and things like that. If you had an extra dollar or two, you might buy a box of rifle shells so you could go and shoot a deer and have a change of diet."

Stan Beech, *CRM aural history*
Beech was born in 1923 and has lived all his life on Quadra Island. A jack-of-all-trades, he has worked at fishing, farming and logging.

Pioneer Pender Harbour fisherman Martin Warnock (right) needs a hand to hold up this big soaker (halibut).

Heavenly Halibut

Serves 4

2 lbs	**halibut fillets**	900 g
2 Tbsp	**onion soup mix**	30 mL
1 cup	**low-fat sour cream**	250 mL

Cut halibut into serving pieces. Mix onion soup mix with sour cream and coat fish pieces.

2 Tbsp	**grated parmesan cheese**	30 mL
1 cup	**bread crumbs**	250 mL
1 Tbsp	**chopped fresh parsley**	15 mL

Preheat oven to 500°F (260°C). Combine cheese, crumbs and parsley. Roll coated fish in cheese mixture.

¼ tsp	**paprika**	1 mL
	butter, melted	

Sprinkle with paprika and butter. Bake for 10–12 minutes.

Jackie MacNaughton

"Catching an abalone is mostly a matter of stealth and speed. Give the gastropod warning that you are there and it tightens its grip on the rock, tightens it so that its potentially delectable foot exerts a force of 400 pounds per square inch. In practice, once this happens, the game is up: the hapless diver cannot pry the abalone loose."

Raymond Sokolov,
Fading Feast

Baked Halibut with Sour Cream

Serves 4

2 lbs	**halibut fillets**	900 g

Place halibut in a shallow baking dish.

	Sauce:	
¼ cup	**mayonnaise**	50 mL
¼ cup	**sour cream**	50 mL
1 Tbsp	**prepared mustard**	15 mL
1 tsp	**dill**	5 mL
1 tsp	**dried parsley flakes**	5 mL
2 Tbsp	**finely minced onion**	30 mL
	salt and pepper to taste	

Preheat oven to 400°F (200°C).
Mix all sauce ingredients together and cover fillets with sauce. Bake for approximately 12 minutes per 1" (2.5 cm) thickness or until fish loses transparency.

Topping:
grated parmesan cheese to taste
grated cheddar cheese to taste

Combine parmesan and cheddar cheese. When fish is nearly done, sprinkle with cheese mixture and broil until cheese bubbles and browns.

Mike Morin

"In 1921 I made a trip on the halibut, eighteen days. We were on the *New England*. Black Bill Taylor was the skipper. She swung twelve dories. Dropping us off was a tricky business. There was a hook on the front end and a hook on the back end, to a boom. You had to make sure the back end was unhooked first or you had disaster. As soon as you hit the water you unhooked. We only went to the steamboat grounds at Cape Scott country, past Triangle until you get to the drop-off. We came in with two hundred and fifty thousand pounds. We got a cent a pound on that trip.
We always carried a jug of coal oil and a hunk of cotton waste. You could tie that on one of the oars and light it when it got dark so the mother ship could see you after dark to pick you up. A lot of the halibut men were 'Newfies'. They're very tough seamen."

Jim Henderson,
CRM aural history

Photo: BCARS.

"The quantity of Fish which we purchased from them [at Nootka] was at least equal to three day's Consumption of both our Ships Companies; and the Variety was far greater than I expected to meet with, according to Captain Cook's account. But it must be Observed, that the Season of the Year was now more favourable for fishing, than at that, at which he was here. The different Kinds with which we were Occasionally supplied, during our stay at Nootka, were, Salmon, Cod, Skate, Halibut, Bream, Trout, with Herrings and Sardines; and also a very fine sort of flat fish (to which I cannot give a name) resembling much in taste and size a Turbot. Our supply of these was however, by no means regular; Sometimes we got more than we could use while sweet; whilst at other times, we were in want for several days together."

James Strange's Journal and Narrative of the Commercial Expedition From Bombay to the Northwest Coast of America, *A. V. Ayyar et al*

Leo Pat Cod

Serves 6

2 lbs	**cod fillets, fresh or frozen**	900 g
	juice of 1 lemon	
½ tsp	**salt**	2 mL
¼ tsp	**pepper**	1 mL

Preheat oven to 425°F (220°C). Cut cod into serving pieces and place in greased baking dish. Sprinkle evenly with lemon juice, then salt and pepper. Bake for 10 minutes or until fish is just barely firm. Remove from oven and set aside.

½ cup	**chopped fresh parsley**	125 mL

Sprinkle parsley on top of fish.

	Meringue:	
7 Tbsp	**mayonnaise**	100 mL
3	**egg whites, stiffly beaten**	3

Gently fold mayonnaise into beaten egg whites. Spread meringue over fish, sealing all around dish.

½ cup	**slivered almonds**	125 mL

Sprinkle meringue with slivered almonds. Return to oven and bake 5–8 minutes longer until topping is puffed and golden. If you have let the first cooking of fish cool down, cook a little longer. Serve immediately.

Gerrie Dinsley

Dr. J. A. Wiborn waves exuberantly as he lands after a successful morning in 1927. Wiborn, the "lone angler" of Zane Grey books, was a founding member of the Tyee Club established in 1925. CRM 10613.

Baked Cod with Spinach & Feta

Serves 4

1 lb	**fresh spinach**	450 g

Cook spinach until wilted. Drain, squeeze and chop coarsely.

¼ cup	**chopped green onion**	50 mL
1	**garlic clove, minced**	1
1 Tbsp	**olive oil**	15 mL

Sauté green onion and garlic in oil until soft.

2 Tbsp	**chopped kalamata (Greek) olives**	30 mL
½ tsp	**oregano**	2 mL
½ cup	**crumbled feta cheese**	125 mL
3 Tbsp	**lemon juice**	45 mL

Stir spinach, olives, oregano, feta cheese and half of the lemon juice into onion and garlic. Mix well.

2 lbs	**cod fillets**	900 g
	salt and pepper to taste	

Preheat oven to 450°F (230°C). Cut cod into 4 pieces ¾" (2 cm) thick. Arrange cod in baking dish in one layer. Sprinkle cod with remaining lemon juice, and salt and pepper. Top with spinach mixture and bake in 450°F (230°C) oven for 12–15 minutes.

Jeanette Taylor

"The house we had bought was not bad, considering what we paid for it. As you went in the door there was the kitchen, a sink, stove and cupboards. The next room was a fair sized living room with the bedroom at the end. There was a big fenced-in yard and on the end of the float there was a wood shed, warehouse and an outhouse. The latter was very convenient because on a rainy day you could fish for cod down through the hole and still keep dry."

Harper Baikie, A Boy and His Axe

Few oyster shells are found in Indian middens along the BC coast because originally the only oysters naturally occurring in the region were the olympic oyster and the rock oyster, both small and scarce. In 1923 that changed forever when a Vancouver doctor named McKechnie decided to set up his son Ian in business cultivating imported Japanese oysters on the mudflats at the head of Pender Harbour. Ian found oysters slow company and gravitated to the nearby pub where he found more immediate rewards baking pies. His untended oysters spawned naturally, spreading as far as Jervis Inlet, twenty miles away. They were eagerly spread around by local residents, with the result that the succulent molluscs are now found wild throughout the Strait of Georgia.

Pan Browned Oysters

Serves 4

½ cup	**butter**	125 mL
½ cup	**oyster juice**	125 mL
4 tsp	**Worcestershire sauce**	20 mL
5 drops	**Tabasco sauce**	5 drops

In a heavy frying pan, melt butter and stir in oyster juice, Worcestershire and Tabasco. Bring to a boil.

16	**oysters**	16

Add oysters and cook, turning gently, until edges begin to turn and they grow plump.

4	**slices French bread, toasted**	4

Place oysters on toast and spoon sauce over top. Serve at once.

Bob Gordon

Tidal flats at Oyster Bay in the head of Pender Harbour, where early oyster cultivating experiments proved a runaway success.

Rod Macaulay's Fried Oysters

Serves 4

½ cup	**flour**	125 mL
¼ cup	**cornmeal**	50 mL
½ tsp	**garlic powder**	2 mL
½ tsp	**onion powder**	2 mL
¼ tsp	**cayenne**	1 mL

Mix all dry ingredients together and set aside.

1	**egg, beaten**	1
1 Tbsp	**milk**	15 mL
24	**small oysters, shucked**	24

Beat egg and milk together. Dip oysters in egg mixture, then in flour mixture.

butter
salt and pepper to taste

Fry oysters in butter until golden brown, approximately 5 minutes on each side. Season to taste.

Rod Macaulay

Clam Patties in Hollandaise Sauce

Makes 10 patties

12	**butter clams, coarsely chopped**	12
1½ cups	**chopped onion**	375mL
4	**egg whites**	4
4 Tbsp	**flour**	50 mL
	salt and pepper to taste	
dash	**poultry seasoning**	dash

Mix clams, onion, egg white, flour and seasonings together and form patties.

	cooking oil	

Heat oil in frying pan. Fry patties until brown on both sides. Keep hot in oven until all are fried.

	Hollandaise Sauce:	
¼ cup	**white vinegar**	50 mL
2 Tbsp	**water**	30 mL
1 Tbsp	**pepper**	15 mL

Boil vinegar, water and pepper until volume is reduced to 2 Tbsp (30 mL).

1 tsp	**tarragon**	5 mL
1 Tbsp	**minced onion**	15 mL
4	**egg yolks, lightly beaten**	4

Add tarragon, onion and yolks and cook over low heat until thickened, stirring constantly.

¼ cup	**butter**	50 mL
squirt	**lemon juice**	squirt

Add butter in three portions, beating thoroughly after each addition, until sauce looks glassy. Add a squirt of lemon juice. Top patties with Hollandaise sauce and serve.

Richard Krentz

"Things were tough going in Depression days. We just survived. I ate so many clams I'd swear my stomach started to go in and out with the tide."

Willie Granlund, *CRM aural history Granlund, a longtime Campbell River logger, led many a logging history program for school groups at the museum.*

Clam Hash

Serves 4

1 Tbsp	**chopped onion**	15 mL
¼ cup	**butter**	50 mL
1½ cups	**cooked, diced potatoes**	375 mL
2 cups	**cooked, chopped clams**	500 mL

Sauté onion in butter. Add potatoes and clams.

2	**eggs, beaten**	2
4 Tbsp	**grated parmesan cheese**	50 mL
6 Tbsp	**milk**	90 mL
	paprika or chopped fresh parsley	

Combine eggs, cheese and milk. Pour over the clams in frying pan. Cover and cook until set. Sprinkle with paprika or parsley. Cut into wedges and serve.

Mary Bennett

"My father and grandfather had a clam co-op on Cortes [Island]. They used to dig clams and they had a clam cannery on the beach. They shipped the canned clams to the Hudson's Bay Company. They were fifteen ounce cans, 'talls'."

Mabel Christensen,
CRM aural history
Mabel Christensen's family were
Cortes Island pioneers.

Working at a clam cannery in Winter Harbour, c. 1907. CRM 19410.

"June 1793—Wherever we had found these fish [mussels] they were sure to afford us a pleasant and palatable fresh meal. Prudence however now directed that we should abstain from them; which, to persons in our situation, especially when detached from the ships, and frequently on a very scanty allowance, was the privation of no small comfort."

The Voyage of George Vancouver 1791–1795, ed. W. Kaye Lamb

Mongo's Mah-h-h-velous Clams

Serves 2–3

1	**onion, chopped**	1
1	**garlic clove, chopped**	1
3 Tbsp	**olive oil**	45 mL
2 Tbsp	**butter**	30 mL

Sauté onion and garlic in oil and butter.

24	**fresh clams, or 1 can baby clams**	24
	oregano to taste	
dash	**cayenne**	dash

Add clams, oregano and cayenne. Continue cooking until clams are done.

8 oz	**fresh pasta, cooked**	225 g

When pasta is cooked *al dente*, toss with clam sauce on a large platter. Add a cup of pasta water to clam mixture if you prefer more juice.

chopped fresh parsley	
freshly ground pepper	

Sprinkle parsley and pepper on top and sit down to a really mah-h-h-vellous meal.

Morgan Ostler

Shrimp & Vegetables in Coconut Milk

Serves 6

2 Tbsp	**peanut oil**	30 mL
2	**onions, thinly sliced**	2
1	**garlic clove, minced**	1
1 tsp	**shrimp paste or fish paste**	5 mL

Heat oil in wok and add onion, garlic and shrimp paste. Stir-fry 5–10 minutes until onions are soft.

2 tsp	**laos** (available in Asian spice stores)	10 mL
1 tsp	**paprika**	5 mL
½	**dried chili pepper, minced**	½
3	**bay leaves**	3
2 tsp	**ground cumin**	10 mL
½ tsp	**pepper**	2 mL
1 tsp	**salt**	5 mL
1 tsp	**honey**	5 mL
drop	**molasses**	drop

Add all seasonings, honey and molasses and stir-fry 2 minutes until a paste forms.

3 cups	**coconut milk**	700 mL
1 tsp	**lemon juice**	5 mL

Slowly add coconut milk and lemon juice. Bring to a boil.

**½ cabbage, shredded or 1 lb (450 g) sliced green beans or
1 lb (450 g) broccoli, broken or 1 lb (450 g) any combination**

Add vegetables and cook 5 minutes until vegetables are just tender.

1 lb	**shrimp**	450 g

Add shrimp and mix well. Stir-fry another 3 minutes. Serve at once.

Estelle Inman

"We had not proceeded far before we heard a dull sound like that often heard from the tide-rips where the current meets and disturbs the waters as like in a boiling cauldron. But as we approached the disturbance, we found it was different from anything we had seen or heard before. As we rested on our oars, we could see that the disturbance was moving up towards us, and that it extended as far as we could see in the direction we were going. The sound had increased and became as like the roar of a heavy rainfall, or hailstorm in water, and we became aware that it was a vast school of herring moving south while millions were seemingly dancing on the surface of the water and leaping in the air. We could sensibly feel them striking against the boat in such vast numbers as to fairly move it as we lay at ease. The leap in the air was so high as to suggest tipping the boat to catch some as they fell back, and sure enough, here and there one would leap into the boat."

Ezra Meeker, *Pioneer Reminiscences of Puget Sound*

*Tyee Man of 1947,
Ray Slocum with his
70½-pound salmon at
Campbell River.
CRM 9993.*

70½ lbs
TYEE SALMON
World's Record on "3/6 Tackle"
TYEE CLUB RECORD
caught by
RAY E. SLOCUM
at
CAMPBELL RIVER, B.C.
July 29, 1947.
D. L "Les" McDonald, Guide
TYEE MAN and 3/6 CHAMPION, 1947.

Seafood Crêpes

Makes 12

Crêpes:

½ cup	**cold water**	125 mL
1 cup	**milk**	250 mL
3	**eggs**	3
½ tsp	**salt**	2 mL
1½ cups	**flour**	375 mL

Beat all crêpe ingredients together with electric mixer. Brush pan with oil, heat over medium-high heat until hot. Pour a scant ¼ cup (50 mL) of batter in middle of pan to make a crêpe 6–7" (17 cm) in diameter. Cook each side about 1 minute until brown and transfer to plate. Repeat, adding wax paper between crêpes.

Filling:

½ cup	**dry sherry**	125 mL
½ cup	**grated swiss cheese**	125 mL
2 cups	**white sauce**	500 mL
1½ cups	**cooked scallops**	375 mL
1½ cups	**cooked crab meat**	375 mL
3 Tbsp	**minced green onion**	45 mL
	salt and pepper to taste	

Add sherry and cheese to white sauce. Combine half the sauce with the seafood and green onion, and season to taste.

Preheat oven to 425°F (220°C). Place seafood mixture on each crêpe, roll up and place in a buttered baking dish. Top with remaining sauce and bake about 20 minutes until heated thoroughly.

Gerrie Dinsley

The proud owner with his prizewinner.
Sayward pioneer Billy Waugh in Vancouver for
an exhibition.
CRM 5869

MEATS

Aboard the Union Steamships

"We went down to eat. There was a couple of loggers came so they sat at the same table. There was the two loggers, a fisherman and myself and the little guy. And after you have lived on the boat all summer it's nice to have a nice meal, so they had braised short ribs, 'beef' they said. So that was fine. So the fisherman says, 'That sounds awful good to me too. I'll guess I'll have it too.' So the loggers, they'd had meat all the time, they weren't very fussy.

By the time we were in Queen Charlotte Sound, it was getting pretty rough when they brought us this beautiful dish. It was a platter, and on that platter there was a cube of meat at least six inches. Then they had vegetables fixed all around it. There was carrots and turnips and potatoes, all done around the meat. And I said,

'Whoop de do!' I said, 'This, this must have been either Paul Bunyan's blue ox or Moby Dick.' Well I got such a dirty look from the loggers, they must have been 'boss' loggers because they really gave me a dirty time. And of course, the fisherman took it right up and said, 'Well,' he said, 'I don't know, we'll see in a minute.'

Well, the sinews were awful, were very pronounced in it, you know. But, you could cut it with your fork. I said, 'That's not Paul Bunyan's blue ox,' I said, 'That is Moby Dick for sure.'

So we enjoyed it you know, and of course, the Scotsman, the head waiter that was downstairs, he'd known me for years. Came over and tapped me on the shoulder and said, 'I want a word with you when you are leaving the dining room.' 'Well,' I said, 'If you wait a minute 'til I get through Moby Dick here, I'll be right with you.' And he said, 'Listen lass, that's enough.'

He said, 'Lass, if you ever say one more thing like that I'm not going to let you back down in that dining room.' And I said, 'Well come on, why don't you.' I said, 'Look how many people had that dish after we were having all the fun about it.' And he said, 'How did you know it was a whale?' 'Well,' I said, 'I didn't come down in the last shower and I do know a little about meat. Anything to have, if that were short ribs of anything it had to be whale in order to produce anything that big and you didn't have a bit of bone in it...' He said, 'You know that we've served that and you are the first person that has detected it and we've served it all summer.'"

Flora Brendeland, *CRM aural history*
Flora Brendeland was a young woman in the 1930s when she took this memorable trip on the Union Steamships.
Photo: BCARS 24881.

The Best Barbecue Sauce

Makes about 3 cups (750 mL)

1 cup	**strong coffee**	250 mL
1 cup	**ketchup**	250 mL
⅓ cup	**vinegar**	75 mL
½ cup	**brown sugar**	125 mL
½ cup	**butter**	125 mL
	juice of ½ lemon	
½ cup	**Worcestershire sauce**	125 mL

Combine and simmer all ingredients for 20 minutes. Store in refrigerator.

Jackie MacNaughton

Lourdes Hospital, Campbell River, was built in 1914. It closed due to financial problems in 1924, but was reopened in 1926 by the Sisters of St. Ann, who operated it for thirty years until a new, larger hospital was built. CRM 309a.

"When we arrived here from Alberta in 1948 the whole country was just full of cattle tracks, anywhere you'd go. The big fire of 1938 wiped the country almost clean here to Courtenay. You could get up on a ridge and as far as you could see in any direction, it was black stumps and black snags. There wasn't a second growth a foot high anywhere. It was willows and brush and miles of grass. There was lots of grazing. My father, George York, unloaded three carloads of stock. The old-timers around here laughed like the dickens. 'You won't have them cows very long. The wild bulls will take them away.' 'Well,' my Dad says, 'we heard all about the wild cattle. We're going to kill them all off.'

The government agreed that the wild cattle would have to go. We were told that at one time there were five hundred head running between Black Creek and the Quinsam River, but there were less than one hundred left when we came in 1948. They got loose from ranches and went wild. The government hired predator hunters to get rid of them, but they hunted them in the summer and it didn't work. We hunted the wild cattle in the winter when the snow was deep. In fact, quite a few people were making a business of hunting them and selling the meat. We got every one but one, and she came in the next summer with Jack Masters' cows. It took us two winters to get rid of the wild cattle."

Virgil and Olive York, *from* Musings *(the CRM Museum Society newsletter),* July 1990

"Farm life was early to bed and early to rise. We were all up in winter by 6:00 a.m.—there were chores to be done before school; usually three cows to be milked and fed and the stable cleaned, chickens to feed, eggs gathered, wood from the wood-shed to be wheeled up and the wood bin filled. We changed our clothes, washed, had breakfast and went to school. We had an unheat-ed room off the kitchen where the milk separator and butter churn were kept, also the water pails and a bench with a basin to wash. In the winter the water would freeze.

In this room, too, any quarters of beef were hung after butcher-ing or large slabs of fish to keep cold. One of our housekeepers had a weird sense of humour. She would make us go out to the washroom every night to say goodnight to the bones before we went to bed. At times they would shine in the night with phospho-rus; this would terrify us, as we thought it was ghosts come to life."

Eve (Willson) Eade
The daughter of Quadra Island home-steaders who arrived in 1887, Eve (Willson) Eade worked in the cannery at Quathiaski Cove from 1937 to 1940. Her memoirs are housed in the CRM Archives.

Beef or Chicken Dijon

Serves 2

4 Tbsp	flour	50 mL
1 tsp	Greek seasoning	5 mL
medallions of beef fillet or boneless, skinless chicken breast		

Combine flour and seasoning. Dredge meat in flour and sauté in pan with a small amount of oil until meat is done. Remove from pan.

2 Tbsp	dry white wine	30 mL
1 Tbsp	butter	15 mL
1 tsp	Dijon mustard	5 mL
2 Tbsp	whipping cream	30 mL

Deglaze pan with wine. Stir in butter, then stir in Dijon mustard. Add cream and reduce to a creamy sauce. Put meat in hot sauce and serve.
Variations: Adding 1 Tbsp (15 mL) pink or green peppercorns makes this a pepper sauce. Or use your imagination and experiment with mustards and other seasonings. The sauce can also be served over vegetables, rice or spuds.

Brad Mielke

Carbonnade of Beef

Serves 6

3 Tbsp	**vegetable oil**	45 mL
3 lbs	**chuck roast or steak, sliced in ½" (1 cm) pieces**	1.4 kg
	salt and pepper to taste	
2	**garlic cloves, crushed**	2
1½ lbs	**onions, thickly sliced**	675 g

Heat oil to sizzling and brown beef slices well. Season meat with salt and pepper and stir in garlic. Remove from pan. Reduce heat and brown onions in the same fat. Layer the meat and onions in a casserole.

1½ cups	**red wine**	375 mL
1 cup	**beef stock**	250 mL
1 Tbsp	**brown sugar**	15 mL
	bouquet garni	

Preheat oven to 350°F (180°C). Mix wine and stock together, stir in sugar and pour into casserole. Poke bouquet garni down into casserole. Cover and cook for 2½ hours. Discard bouquet garni.

2 Tbsp	**cornstarch**	30 mL
2 Tbsp	**vinegar**	30 mL

Mix cornstarch with vinegar and stir into sauce to thicken.

Thelma Silkens

Growing Up in Port Neville

"The kitchen was the main room in our big log house, the centre of all activities. It was a huge room with a table large enough, with added leaves, to seat about sixteen adults. There would also be an extra table for large gatherings at Christmas. The stove was a huge black monster with nickel trim and 'Albion' printed across the oven door in nickel letters. The warming oven was huge, and full of all manner of things— from dripping pot to sadirons. Under the warming oven were metal gadgets that folded up against the back, on which to set the tea and coffee pots. We took great pride in keeping our 'Albion' as clean as possible, and bear grease was rubbed into it vigorously to keep it shining. The only drawback to this was the odour that wafted through the air for a few minutes until it burned off. Because our 'Albion' also heated a good portion of the downstairs area, it swallowed up an enormous amount of wood every day. To have a good fire for baking many golden loaves of bread as well as the other cooking for a large family, good wood was needed.

Edith (Hansen) Bendickson

This passage comes from an article published in 1966 in the Campbell River Courier, *in which Edith (Hansen) Bendickson remembers her childhood in Port Neville during the 1920s and '30s. Her father, Hans Hansen, established the Port Neville Post Office in 1895.*

Herbed Lamb Stew

Serves 6

1½ lbs	**lamb stew meat, cubed**	675 g
2 Tbsp	**cooking oil**	30 mL

Brown meat in hot oil.

1	**clove garlic, minced**	1
1	**bay leaf**	1
2	**beef bouillon cubes**	2
½ tsp	**thyme**	2 mL
½ tsp	**oregano**	2 mL
½ tsp	**marjoram**	2 mL
	salt and pepper to taste	
2 cups	**water**	500 mL

Add seasonings and water to meat. Bring to a boil, reduce heat and simmer for 1 hour, covered.

4	**carrots, sliced**	4
4	**celery stalks, sliced**	4
2	**onions, cut in quarters**	2

Add vegetables and simmer another 30 minutes or until vegetables are tender.

½ cup	**sour cream**	125 mL
¼ cup	**flour**	50 mL
2 Tbsp	**water**	30 mL

In a separate bowl, combine sour cream, flour and water. Take ½ cup (125 mL) hot broth from the stew, add it to the sour cream mixture, stir well and return the sour cream mixture to the stew. Cook and stir until thickened.

Bruce Saunders

Slaughter'd Verse

Slaughter brought some dandy lambs
They came from Denman Isle,
And people that live hereabouts
Enjoyed it with a smile.
The simple reason of this is—
An obliging gent is he.
No order is too small to cut
For his delivery.

*Comox Argus,
November 26, 1925*

Lamb Kebabs

Serves 6

Marinate for 30 minutes

1 lb	**bacon**	450 g
4 lbs	**lamb, deboned**	1.8 kg
60	**fresh mushrooms**	60

Cut bacon into 1" (2.5 cm) squares and set aside. Cut lamb into 1" (2.5 cm) cubes, place in glass or ceramic bowl.

	Marinade:	
1	**lemon**	1
1 tsp	**rosemary**	5 mL
1 tsp	**thyme**	5 mL
3	**large garlic cloves, pressed**	3
⅓ cup	**olive oil**	75 mL

With vegetable peeler, remove the lemon peel, mince and sprinkle over lamb. Juice the lemon, combine lemon juice with remaining marinade ingredients and pour over lamb. Let sit for 30 minutes.

String skewers beginning with a piece of bacon, mushroom, bacon, then lamb cube. Before cooking, brush remaining marinade over the kebabs and broil or barbecue 10–12 minutes each side.

Stephanie Tipple

"Lagoon Cove, Cracroft Island—In a part of the Province like this where people are a hundred miles or more from a butcher, one regrets that the government should be so asinine as to pass a law that the bottling of venison is illegal. This is bad enough, but when they take off the bounty on cougar and wolves which are destroying countless deer and chasing them out of many districts where they used to be plentiful, one wonders whether the people who are responsible for these pitiful laws can be sane."

Francis Barrow's journal,
August 21, 1933.

Herbert Joyce watches Chappie Bigold aboard the "Woolsey" at the Alfred Joyce farm on Quadra Island, 1914.
CRM 4447.

Green Chili

Serves 8

2 lbs	cubed pork	900 g
1	onion, diced	1
2	garlic cloves, minced	2

Remove all fat from pork. Heat a bit of oil in a pan and cook pork until brown. Add onion and garlic and cook until limp. Drain off grease.

2 Tbsp	chili powder	30 mL
	salt and pepper to taste	
28 oz	canned, chopped tomatoes	796 mL
2	jalapeno peppers, finely diced	2
1	small tin green chilies, diced	1

Combine remaining ingredients and add to pork. Bring to a boil, reduce heat and simmer, covered, for up to 3 hours. Serve in a bowl over rice, with warm tortillas on the side.

Bill Harrison

"Most loggers in the dining room ... had table manners, but sometimes you'd run into the odd 'pig'. When I worked in a camp at Bowser in 1936 ... this table I was sitting at, I couldn't believe what happened. This one 'pig' he was always reaching instead of asking. Usually someone would jab his arm with a fork to send him a message.

The guy down the line from me asked for the pork chops and this big platter of pork chops in gravy had to go by this 'pig.' He stopped it here because he wanted some and he picked up each chop and looked at the bottom side to see how they were done. Eventually he took what he wanted and passed them on to the guy next to him who originally wanted them. By this time this guy was absolutely furious. So when he got the platter, he just stepped out of his seat and went behind the 'pig' and said, 'You want pork chops, I'll give you pork chops' and he dumped the whole platter of meat and gravy on the 'pig's' head."

Willie Granlund,
CRM aural history

Sunnyside Farm, Quadra Island, with "Peg" in the foreground. From Rob Yeatman's album. CRM 6296.

Opposite:
Butcher dressing a hog at Bloedel, Stewart & Welch logging camp, 1917.
CRM 18879.

"When Paul Bunyan lived on the West Coast, he worked at the Big Pumpkin Creek logging camp. The cookhouse there was so big the men were given 'starter' meals of steak and eggs when they first went in so they could make it to the tables for the main course. Each table was served by a flunkie who wore roller skates. If a flunkie really hustled, he could make it all the way around a table in twenty-four hours. Cleaning up was done by teams of red-headed dishwashers who could wash and stack thirty thousand plates an hour. Overseeing all this was the cook, who rode around on a motorcycle shouting orders through a megaphone."

Tom Henry, Paul Bunyan on the West Coast

Mexican Meat Pie

Serves 8–12

2 lbs	**ground beef**	900 g
	finely chopped onion to taste	
2	**garlic cloves, crushed**	2

Sauté meat, onion and garlic in frying pan and cook over low heat until meat loses its red colour. Drain off all fat.

2 cups	**tomato sauce**	500 mL
2 cups	**corn niblets, canned or frozen**	500 mL
½	**green pepper, chopped**	½
1 tsp	**chili powder**	5 mL
1¾ tsp	**cumin**	8 mL
dash	**tabasco sauce**	dash
1 tsp	**salt**	5 mL
1 tsp	**sugar**	5 mL

Stir in tomato sauce, corn, green pepper and seasonings. Bring to a boil and simmer for 2 minutes.

	Topping:	
1 cup	**cornmeal**	250 mL
¾ cup	**milk**	175 mL
1¼ cups	**flour, sifted and remeasured**	300 mL
2½ tsp	**baking powder**	12 mL
1 tsp	**salt**	5 mL
½ cup	**shortening**	125 mL
¼ cup	**sugar**	50 mL
1	**egg, beaten**	1
¾ cup	**milk**	175 mL

You need four bowls for mixing. In first bowl combine cornmeal and milk. In second bowl, sift and remeasure flour, stir in baking powder and salt. In third bowl, cream shortening and sugar until creamy. In fourth bowl beat egg and milk. To the shortening mixture, add alternately the flour mixture and egg mixture, then add the cornmeal mixture.

⅔ cup	**grated cheddar cheese**	150 mL

Stir in cheese. Preheat oven to 350°F (180°C).
Spread meat mixture in a 9x13" (23x33 cm) baking dish; spoon topping over meat. Bake for 45–60 minutes.

salsa

sour cream

Serve with salsa and/or sour cream.

Bill Harrison

While no match for Paul Bunyan's cook house at Big Pumpkin Creek, this floating humdinger complete with skylights was the pride of its crew. VPL 1477.

Penang Beef Balls

Serves 4

1 lb	**lean ground beef**	450 g
½ cup	**flour**	125 mL
	cooking oil	

Shape beef into balls and dust with flour. Brown the balls in hot oil in a wok or frying pan until evenly cooked. Set aside on absorbent paper.

3 Tbsp	**red curry paste**	45 mL

In remaining oil, stir-fry red curry paste for several minutes over low heat to prevent sticking.

1½ cups	**coconut milk**	375 mL

Add coconut milk and stir.

1½ Tbsp	**bottled Thai fish sauce**	23 mL
2 Tbsp	**ground peanuts or crunchy peanut butter**	30 mL
1 Tbsp	**sugar**	15 mL

Add fish sauce, peanuts and sugar. Taste, add extra fish sauce or sugar as needed, then return beef balls to sauce and simmer for 5 minutes or more.

2 Tbsp	**fresh chopped basil, mint or cilantro**	30 mL

Garnish with herbs and serve.

Jeanette Taylor

"In my long years of logging that had to be the best camp I ever worked in. There was more food on the table than was possible for the crew to eat. Coming off a farm we had lots to eat but not much variety. I spent a lot of time looking at all the meat, vegetables, fruits and pies which I could not eat or I would bust a gut. The bunk houses were as modern as any at that time. There were eight men to a bunkhouse, with clean sheets every week, good showers and board walks to the cookhouse and office. There was even a ball park to play soccer or baseball. Through the years I have read many articles on how tough the camp conditions were in those times. My experience was very good. I have been at camps from Seymour Inlet and south, and never have I seen a camp as poor as some writers make out they were. It is more likely they were fired and figured it is a good way to get even with the camp.

I have had several camps of my own and I am proud to say the food was always good and there was lots of it. While we are on the subject of cooks and camps, in the 1960–70s there was a deal going that if you hired a man and he worked thirty days you could not fire him unless the union, the labour relations people and everybody else who thought they had any authority got into the act. I soon developed a system of watching the cooks very closely. The first three weeks they cooked it seemed they could do no wrong. As time went on they would start to get careless and that was when you had to get rid of them. If they ever got past the thirty days you were stuck with them for life.

I do not remember how many cooks I fired in a twenty year period but somehow I got the nickname 'Can the cook'."

Harper Baikie,
A Boy and His Axe

Locomotive pulling a load of logs rumbles past the cookhouse in the days of steam. BCARS 53605.

Living off the land: wild pigeon bounty.
Sunnyside Farm, Quadra Island, c. 1915.
CRM 6228

GAME

Baked Grouse

Makes 1 grouse

1	grouse	1
	flour	
	salt and pepper to taste	
	oil	

Cut the grouse into serving pieces. Dredge with flour seasoned with salt and pepper. In frying pan, brown grouse in oil and place in a casserole.

1 Tbsp	chopped onion	15 mL
1 cup	sliced mushrooms	250 mL

Sauté onion and mushrooms and add to casserole.

1 Tbsp	butter	15 mL
1 Tbsp	flour	15 mL
½ cup	chicken stock	125 mL
½ cup	dry white wine	125 mL
	salt and pepper to taste	

Preheat oven to 350°F (180°C).

In a frying pan, melt butter. Add flour and stir to blend. Mix in stock, wine, salt and pepper. Pour sauce into casserole. Cover and bake for 1 hour.

Jacquie Gordon

Algernon Lloyd, before 1914. "Algy" went overseas during World War One. CRM 6470.

Game Marinade

Makes enough for a 4–5 pound (2 kg) roast
Marinate 3–5 days

2	onions, sliced	2
1	carrot, sliced	1
2–3	whole cloves	2–3
3–4	peppercorns, cracked	3–4
1	bay leaf	1
2	sprigs fresh parsley	2
2 cups	red wine	500 mL
1 Tbsp	cider vinegar	15 mL
3	garlic cloves, crushed	3
3 Tbsp	olive oil	45 mL
2	juniper berries (optional)	2

Combine all ingredients in large crock or other non-metal container. Coat meat in marinade and hold it off bottom of container with inverted saucer. Marinate 3–5 days, turning occasionally and stirring marinade.

Pat Luoma

"My Dad used to go hunting 'up north' in November when we were kids. We used to think 'up north' was near the North Pole, so we gave Daddy our letter to Santa to give to him."
Jacquie Gordon

"In 1948, I had a logging job up the Oyster River. One day I was sitting at the landing, waiting for the truck to be loaded, and I watched blue grouse crossing the road about three hundred feet away. They were massed in some kind of migration, a flock of one hundred and fifty to two hundred walking through the slash and heading into the timber in the Oyster River canyon. In those days, there were all kinds of grouse."
Norm Hinch

Agricultural show at Sayward, BC, c. 1925. The fair drew participants from throughout the area and nearby islands. CRM 5865.

In July 1910, the Honourable Price Ellison, Chief Commissioner of Lands for the Government of British Columbia, led an expedition to explore the possibility of developing the Buttle Lake area as a provincial park. After Crown Mountain had been climbed and named and their survey completed, the members of the expedition celebrated with a feast at Buttle's Lake:

"We are to have a grand feast tonight in honour of our leaving the lake and Scotty Twaddle starts early to prepare it. He uses up all of our delicacies which we have been saving for a special occasion. From now on until we reach civilization, we are to live on bacon, beans and rice."

The following is the official menu for this great occasion:

Menu
Ox Tail Soup, Clam Chowder
Chutney, Pickles
Lake Trout, River Trout, Sardines
Blue Grouse with Mushroom sauce
Corn off the Cob, French Peas, Beans
Custard, Pineapple, sliced Peaches
Tea, Coffee
Cheese, Nuts, Raisins
Port, Champagne, Lemonade
Pipes

Harry Johnson, *Journal of BC Exploratory Survey Trip into Buttle Lake region, 1910.*

Wild Duck à l'Orange

Serves 8

4	**wild ducks**	4
	salt	
2	**oranges, unpeeled**	2
2	**apples, unpeeled**	2
2	**onions, peeled**	2
2	**garlic cloves, halved**	2
8	**peppercorns**	8

Preheat oven to 425°F (220°C).

Wash and dry ducks, sprinkle inside with salt. Cut fruit and onions into eighths and divide fruit, onions, garlic and peppercorns into four. Stuff each duck. Close with skewers. Tie legs together and place in large roasting pan.

½ cup	**burgundy**	125 mL

Pour burgundy over ducks and roast for 20 minutes. Reduce heat to 350°F (180°C). Baste ducks and cover with foil. Roast 1 hour. Uncover and baste, spoon off all juices and reserve. Roast uncovered 15 minutes.

¾ cup	**orange marmalade**	175 mL

Spread ducks with marmalade. Bake another 15 minutes. Remove ducks to serving platter and keep warm. Pour off pan juices and add to reserved juices.

2½ Tbsp	**duck oil**	38 mL
3 Tbsp	**flour**	45 mL
1 cup	**pan juices**	250 mL

Spoon off oil from juices and return 2½ Tbsp (38 mL) to pan. Stir in flour, add pan juices, cook and stir until thick. Add more pan juice until gravy is of desired consistency.

2	**oranges, cut in rounds**	2

To serve, cut ducks in half. Discard stuffing. Garnish with orange slices and serve with wild and brown rice.

Jacquie Gordon

Fort Rupert

In the spring of 1849, the Hudson's Bay company established a fort, principally to extract coal, near the current town of Port Hardy on north-eastern Vancouver Island. This was one of the first European settlements on Vancouver Island and one where people of many different nationalities came to live.

At the fort were one hundred English, French-Canadian, Hawaiian, Scottish and Kwakwa̲ka'wakw people, who found the conditions appalling, and the company brass unsympathetic. The drafty log dwellings comprised a single room, with crushed clam shell for flooring, and as one occupant recalled there were "bugs innumerable, fleas without limit."

Annie Muir was in her forty-eighth year when she and her extended family were hired in Scotland to work the mine at Fort Rupert. Her feisty determination to resist company food restrictions and to support her son Andrew in the first labour strike in British Columbia history, is recorded in Andrew's diary:

"Mrs. McGregor, Mrs. Smith and Sister went outside in the afternoon when there was two deer given to them which they skinned and put into two baskets to carry them into the house. On entering the Fort gate, Blenkinsop and Bredmore, [Fort managers] in a ruffian like manner, seized and tore the basket off her back and would not allow her to bring the meat into the house but said his trader would trade it and would send it to them and whatever he paid for it he would charge to their husbands'

accounts. When mother went out, (I was really surprised for I never saw her in such a state. She would rather suffer anything than breed a disturbance. But they had trodden too much on good nature.) she boldly said she was a free woman and had no meat from the company, therefore she should buy her meat from the best and cheapest market. After a little more altercations, the baskets with the women carrying them came over to the house triumphant over the cowardly rascals who could attack a woman—two to one."

Fishermen's Lodge on the Oyster River. The lodge was built around 1921 by Mrs. Walter Whyte, who obtained the six-acre site from the Comox Logging Company for a reported sum of $100. CRM 10189.

Roast Venison

Serves 8–10

	venison roast	
	salt and pepper	
	grated dried ginger	
2 Tbsp	**melted butter**	30 mL
3	**bacon strips**	3
1	**onion**	1
	whole cloves	

Preheat oven to 325°F (160°C).

Rub roast with salt, pepper and ginger. Place in pan and pour butter over roast. Lay bacon strips on top. Peel onion and stick with cloves, place in roasting pan.

Roast for 20 minutes per pound for rare meat. Baste frequently.

2 Tbsp	**butter**	30 mL
½ cup	**red wine**	125 mL
2–3	**juniper berries** (optional)	2–3

Half an hour before roast is done, add butter, wine and juniper berries to pan.

dash	**Worcestershire sauce**	dash
	mace to taste	
	flour	

After removing roast, season the sauce with Worcestershire and mace. Thicken with flour to make gravy.

Margaret Margetts

" I grew up in Union Bay and my daddy, Harry Glover, hunted all types of birds. For several years he and a group of friends rented a seiner and travelled to Knight Inlet to hunt for ducks, brant and Canada geese. Dad and his cousin Wilf carved their own beautiful decoys to use on the hunt. When he got home, we all got busy and plucked the birds. Nothing was wasted, the down was used for quilts and pillows and the soft feathers for cushions. After the birds were cooked, the goose grease was used to make poultices for chest colds and for waterproofing boots.

Years later when we were married, Robert would arrive home from his annual two-week hunting trip to the prairies and present me with a sack full of prairie chickens, ducks and geese. I shivered in the garage with feathers up my nose as I dutifully plucked the lot and then gave duck dinner parties. Some years later, after I became liberated, I insisted he help with the plucking. Soon the birds began arriving from the prairies plucked, plastic-wrapped and ready for the freezer or pan!"
Jacquie Gordon

At the end of Seaview Road you will find Seaview Farms, a 160-acre ranch where Frank Schuman raises fallow deer. The herd numbers nearly three hundred animals. These deer were originally brought to British Columbia by a British nobleman and installed on James and Sidney Islands near Victoria. They are smaller than our Island deer.

A 177-pound buck shot at Haskins Farm, Quadra Island, October 1919. CRM 6276.

Anna "Granny" Joyce decapitates a chicken with experienced prowess.
CRM 5684

POULTRY

"My brother Charlie (now living in Powell River) was born and lived for twelve years at Cape Mudge. He could tell some tales, about life there. He was not allowed to hunt with a gun so he would take 'Old Sophie,' the horse, and ride bareback up to the long swamp with a slingshot and a gunny sack and come back with his limit of what they called 'fool hens,' not sure what type of grouse that was but you could knock one off the branch and the rest would just sit there and watch so you could get in another shot and so on, hence the name 'fool'."

Virginia McPhee, *granddaughter of Quadra Island pioneers Alfred and Anna Joyce, CRM aural history*

Pineapple Chicken

Serves 2
Marinate for 2–3 hours

1 lb	chicken	450 g

Cut chicken into bite-sized pieces.

	Marinade:	
2 tsp	scotch or rye	10 mL
2 Tbsp	dark soy sauce	30 mL
1 tsp	sugar	5 mL

Combine all marinade ingredients and marinate chicken pieces for 2–3 hours.

1	large garlic clove, minced	1
3 slices	fresh ginger root, slivered	3 slices
2 Tbsp	peanut or corn oil	30 mL
	pineapple chunks to taste	

Sauté garlic and ginger in oil over medium-high heat. Add chicken and marinade. Cook for 7–8 minutes, stirring frequently. Add pineapple.

	Sauce:	
1 Tbsp	cornstarch	15 mL
2 tsp	soy sauce	10 mL
	salt and pepper to taste	
3 oz	pineapple juice	85 mL

Combine sauce ingredients. Add to chicken and cook for another 2–3 minutes. Serve hot with rice.

Larry Chen

Red Curry Chicken

Serves 3–4

12 oz	**boneless chicken breast**	350 g
2 Tbsp	**oil**	30 mL

Cut chicken into bite-sized pieces and cook with oil in a wok.

1 pkg	**red curry paste**	1 pkg
1	**red bell pepper, chopped**	1
1	**onion, sliced**	1
14 oz	**coconut milk**	398 mL
10 oz	**bamboo shoots, drained**	284 mL

Add curry paste, red pepper, onion, coconut milk and bamboo shoots. Cook 10–15 minutes until thick.

1	**stalk Thai holy basil**	1

Add basil to chicken. Serve over hot cooked rice.

Jeanne Ralston

"For the [Joyce] family picnic at Drew Harbour, Granny Joyce would go out and kill seven chickens."

Virginia McPhee,
CRM aural history

Mary Henry in front of the Henry homestead at Sayward, 1914. Old railway ties from a Hastings Company line were used to build the shed.
CRM 5868

Super Chicken

Serves 4

	Sauce:	
1 cup	**sour cream**	250 mL
10 oz	**condensed cream of mushroom soup**	284 mL
¼ cup	**light cream**	50 mL
	salt and white pepper to taste	
pinch	**thyme**	pinch
pinch	**sage**	pinch

Combine all sauce ingredients in a double boiler and simmer 5–10 minutes.

1	**bunch green onions, chopped**	1
	butter or oil	

Sauté onion in butter or oil. Add to sauce.

4 oz	**mushrooms, sliced**	112 g
1	**bay leaf**	1
1 cup	**dry sherry**	250 mL

Sauté mushrooms in the same pan. Add bay leaf and sherry, simmer for 5 minutes and add to sauce.

3	**chicken breasts, skinned and cut in half (boneless or bone-in)**	3
	cooking oil	
¼ cup	**slivered almonds**	50 mL

Brown chicken in oil until golden. Preheat oven to 300°F (150°C). Arrange chicken in ovenproof casserole, pour on sauce, and sprinkle almonds on top. Cover and bake for 1½ hours.

chopped fresh parsley

Garnish with parsley and serve over hot cooked rice.

Jay Stewart

Opulent Chicken

Serves 4

4	**whole chicken breasts**	4
	paprika, salt and pepper to taste	
4 oz	**butter**	112 g
14 oz	**artichoke hearts, in water**	398 mL

Split chicken breasts, slather with paprika, salt and pepper. Heat a skillet and sauté chicken in half of the butter. Place chicken and artichoke hearts in a casserole.

8 oz	**mushrooms, sliced**	225 g
pinch	**tarragon**	pinch
3 Tbsp	**flour**	45 mL
⅓ cup	**sherry**	75 mL
1½ cups	**chicken broth**	375 mL

In the same skillet, heat the rest of the butter and sauté mushrooms. Season with tarragon and sprinkle flour in. Add sherry and chicken broth, and simmer 5 minutes. Preheat oven to 375°F (190°C). Pour sauce over chicken. Cover and bake for 45 minutes.

Jay Stewart

"At lunch time, we have dried salmon or dried clams in the wintertime. In summertime, we have everything: fresh salmon, halibut, flounder, cod, hair seals, clams, cockles, horse clams, fruits and potatoes, but we don't eat all the different kinds of roots in the summertime. We eat all the different kinds of ducks, but we don't eat sea gulls, cormorants, and loons. They are too tough and too hard to pluck. I guess we would if we didn't have anything else to eat, but we always did. We eat eagles in the wintertime, when they get fat eating fish. We don't eat frogs, nor do we eat snakes. We are afraid of them and won't touch them unless we have to. Some of us run away from them, and some kill them. I know I kill them myself. There is a story of a man who died with a frog inside him, but I didn't know him."

Clellan S. Ford, *Smoke from Their Fires: The Life of a Kwakiutl Chief*

Thai Chicken & Noodles

Serves 3
Marinate 30 minutes

2	**chicken breasts, chopped**	2
2 Tbsp	**sherry**	30 mL

Marinate chicken in sherry for 30 minutes.

3 Tbsp	**vegetable oil**	45 mL
8	**garlic cloves, minced**	8
6	**shallots, minced**	6
4	**red serrano chilies**	4
1 tsp	**anchovy paste**	5 mL
	salt to taste	

Heat oil and sauté garlic, shallots, chilies, anchovy paste and salt. Add chicken and sauté.

3 Tbsp	**tomato paste**	45 mL
2 tsp	**peanut butter**	10 mL
2 Tbsp	**sugar**	30 mL
1 Tbsp	**bottled Thai fish sauce**	15 mL
½ cup	**water**	125 mL

Add tomato paste, peanut butter, sugar, fish sauce and water. Cook and stir until of a sauce consistency.

12 oz	**vermicelli**	350 g

Cook vermicelli and toss with sauce until well coated.

½ cup	**bean sprouts**	125 mL
¼ cup	**red pepper flakes**	50 mL
2 Tbsp	**chopped peanuts**	30 mL

Garnish with bean sprouts, red pepper and peanuts, and serve.

Jeanne Ralston

Chicken Wings

Serves 6

3 lbs	**chicken wings**	1.4 kg
2	**eggs, beaten**	2
1 cup	**flour**	250 mL

Preheat oven to 350°F (180°C).

Cut wings in half and discard tips. Dip in egg, then in flour. Place in roasting pan and bake until golden.

	Sauce:	
3 Tbsp	**light soy sauce**	45 mL
3 Tbsp	**water**	45 mL
1 cup	**white sugar**	250 mL
½ cup	**vinegar**	125 mL

Mix all sauce ingredients together and heat or microwave until sugar dissolves. Pour sauce over wings and bake 30 minutes, basting occasionally.

Margaret Morris

The Yeatman family, Quadra Island, Christmas 1915. Rob Yeatman (at left) was an amateur photographer whose hobby yielded a rich historical record of islanders' daily life.
CRM 6307.

Cheddar Chicken

Serves 4

1	roasting chicken	1

Leave chicken whole or cut into sections. Place in roasting pan.

½ cup	sliced mushroom	125 mL
10 oz	condensed cream of mushroom soup	284 mL
½ tsp	minced garlic	2 mL
1½ tsp	curry powder	7 mL
½ tsp	pepper	2 mL

In a separate bowl, mix next five ingredients together gently.

1 cup	dry white wine	250 mL
2 cups	grated medium cheddar cheese	500 mL
1 Tbsp	paprika	15 mL

Slowly add wine to sauce. Pour over chicken in pan. Sprinkle cheese over chicken and sprinkle paprika on top.

Preheat oven to 325°F (160°C). Bake chicken for 30 minutes per pound. When chicken browns, cover with foil for remainder of baking time.

Bruce Saunders

Beginning an island tradition, the first community picnic was held at Cape Mudge Lighthouse, c. 1898., CRM 7493.

Mustard Lemon Chicken

Serves 4–6

4	**chicken breasts, skin on**	4
	Sauce:	
2 Tbsp	**Dijon mustard**	30 mL
1	**garlic clove, minced**	1
1 Tbsp	**tarragon**	15 mL
	juice of 1 lemon	

Preheat oven to 325°F (160°C). Mix all sauce ingredients together and paint chicken breasts. Bake for 35 minutes or until done and slightly browned.

To barbecue: Place skin side up on rack 6" (15 cm) over medium heat. Cook for about 30 minutes, painting on more sauce a couple of times. Turn skin side down and cook for 10 more minutes, or until done.

Bruce Saunders

"My Dear Roy:
So tomorrow is to be your wedding day! We will be thinking of you and Mabel all day. I suppose [blank] and Barbara will be at the wedding. Well, I certainly wish you both all the happiness in life, may your **love** for each other never grow cold! See to it that you are kind and thoughtful about your wife. I believe that men are usually selfish, and they seem to think if they provide their wives with the necessaries of life, the wives should be satisfied and grateful. They forget that most of us were making our living before marriage, and could continue to do so— what we married for was love, and not for a **living**. The men made us believe that we would always be kindly treated and no doubt they believed it themselves, but most of them **cheat** their wives out of the kind treatment. Don't let me ever hear of you scolding because your meals are not ready, or you can't find your necktie. Take care of your own necktie, and put it in its place. But, whatever you do, don't **swear**—that is one of the meanest things a man can do."
from a letter written by **E. Marlatt** *to her son, dated March 20, 1904. The Marlatt family later came to live on Marina Island, off Cortes Island.*

"On this occasion I deemed it expedient, that those employed on boat service should be supplied with an additional quantity of wheat and potable soup, sufficient to afford them two hot meals every day during their absence; and, in consequence of their being much exposed to the prevailing inclement weather, an additional quantity of spirits."

The Voyage of George Vancouver 1791–1795, ed. W. Kaye Lamb

Radienber Sangha's Chicken Curry

Serves 8

2 chickens, or 24 legs, or 4 whole breasts

Skin chicken and cut into serving size pieces. (Do not use wings.) Legs and thighs may be left whole. Cut each breast into 4 pieces.

¼ cup	**oil**	50 mL
1	**whole bulb garlic, minced**	1
5	**onions, minced**	5

Heat oil and cook garlic and onion until well browned.

2 Tbsp	**salt**	30 mL
	pepper to taste	
2 Tbsp	**turmeric**	30 mL
1½ Tbsp	**cayenne**	23 mL
¾ cup	**tomato paste**	175 mL

Add seasonings and tomato paste and continue cooking for 5 minutes. Add more oil if mixture is sticking. Add chicken.

2 cups	**water**	500 mL

Add ½ cup (125 mL) of the water and stir to coat the chicken with sauce. Cover and simmer 1 hour, *or* bake at 350°F (180°C) for 1 hour. Add remaining water and stir. If sauce is too thick, add more water. Simmer another hour.

½ cup	**chopped fresh cilantro**	125 mL

Sprinkle cilantro over top. Serve with hot cooked rice or roti.

Radienber Sangha

*Sheringham Point lighthouse, perched atop a rocky knoll on the Strait of Juan de Fuca
near Sooke. Food author Anita Stewart was so impressed with
BC lightkeepers' skill at producing varied menus with limited ingredients she collected
their recipes in* The Lighthouse Cookbook.

There is always time for delighting in blossoms.
Mrs. James Nixon among flowering fruit trees
on Twin Islands, 1913.
CRM 5916

DESSERTS

Pumpkins Rolling in the Sea

Among the first Europeans to move into the Campbell River area in the 1880s was an Irishman, Fred Nunns. A bachelor, Nunns kept a diary which is now held in the Provincial Archives of British Columbia. In it his endearing, sometimes cantankerous personality shines through his terse entries.

Like many settlers, Fred grew extra produce at his riverside homestead, providing vital pioneer commodities which were much prized in logging camps. The adventures encountered in transporting a canoe load of pumpkins to a camp at Granite Bay on Quadra Island is a humorous tale which inspired a popular puppet play at the Campbell River Museum. Based on his diary account, a lively cast of characters includes a sinuous-fingered thieving "tide" puppet.

Leaving his homestead on the banks of the Campbell River, Fred set off with his canoe loaded with pumpkins and squash—a trip of 35 kilometres paddling over very rough water. A miscalculation of the tide brought Fred to the infamous Seymour Narrows, one of the most noted marine hazards on the coast, when the tide was "rushing through like a mill race." Planning to safely wait out the change of tide, Fred made camp for the night and unwittingly endangered his precious cargo.

"Thursday, October 23, 1890: This morning 2:00 a.m. I got up to put fresh logs on the fire then went to look at canoe. Found tide in, going out had [capsized] her on a rock and the pumpkins and squash were floating all around. Lit a fire near canoe and collected them. Found I had lost nine pumpkins and twenty-four squash. Got through Narrows at daybreak and had a hard pull up to Grant's where I arrived 11:00 a.m., wet through, as it had been raining all morning. Found Grant was not there but expected in afternoon. S.S. *Danube* turned up 4:00 p.m., with Grant and a lot of freight which I helped them to get ashore."

Fred waited through a night of the loggers' freight day revelry. "The men got a lot of liquor and had a regular drunken night of it. I never got a wink of sleep."

The next morning Fred sold his produce noting that he got 37 cents each for the pumpkins and 12 cents each for the squash. With the funds he bought "barley for my hogs, one box cartridges, three large bottles of sauce and about twenty books" before he set off once again to paddle his way home through the tidal rip of Seymour Narrows.

Ploughing with Old Bess and Mr. Bryant's horse, at "Sunnyside," the Yeatman farm on Quadra Island, 1911. CRM 6094.

Apple Slice

Serves 6

Crust:		
½ cup	**butter or margarine**	125 mL
¾ cup	**flour**	175 mL
½ cup	**quick or slow-cooking rolled oats**	125 mL
2 Tbsp	**sugar**	30 mL

Melt butter and stir in flour, oats and sugar. Press evenly into 8" (20 cm) baking pan. Preheat oven to 350°F (180°C).

Filling:		
2	**eggs**	2
1 cup	**brown sugar**	250 mL
1 tsp	**vanilla**	5 mL
2 cups	**diced apple**	500 mL
¼ cup	**chopped almonds or raisins**	50 mL

Beat eggs until thick and creamy. Stir in sugar, vanilla, apple and almonds.

½ cup	**flour**	125 mL
1 tsp	**baking powder**	5 mL
¼ tsp	**nutmeg**	1 mL

Sift flour, baking powder and nutmeg together and stir into egg mixture. Spread filling over crust and bake for 30 minutes.

This recipe can be doubled and baked in a 9x13" (23x33 cm) pan for 45 minutes.

	whipped cream	

Serve with whipped cream.

Jessica Madsen

Indian Ice Cream

The soapberry (*soopalallie* in Chinook) is a small, sour, orange berry that prefers a fairly dry climate, yet aboriginal groups living near the raincoast have enjoyed soapberries for centuries by trading with their inland neighbours. In fact soapberries are traditionally one of the most widely used fruits throughout BC—because you can make Indian Ice Cream from it.

The soapberries are macerated with sugar, then whipped into a froth to make the "ice cream"—a distinctively tart–sweet concoction often served on special occasions, with special utensils. Before there were egg beaters, aboriginal people whipped the berries with salal branches or cedar bark.

With soapberry froth, it was all right to play with your food. Indian ice cream was a party treat, eaten with great merriment and tossed around in fun. The Gitksan people even have a word for it: *'niist*—to smear with soapberry foam.

Pumpkin Cake Roll

Serves 8–10

Chill 30 minutes

Grease a 15x10x1" (38x25x3 cm) pan, line it with wax paper, grease well again and flour.

	Batter:	
3	**eggs**	3
¾ cup	**sugar**	175 mL
⅔ cup	**cooked pumpkin**	150 mL

Beat eggs on high speed for 5 minutes. Gradually add sugar, beating well. Add pumpkin and blend.

¾ cup	**flour**	175 mL
1 tsp	**baking powder**	5 mL
2 tsp	**cinnamon**	10 mL
1 tsp	**grated dried ginger**	5 mL
½ tsp	**nutmeg**	2 mL
½ tsp	**salt**	2 mL

Combine all dry ingredients. Add dry ingredients to pumpkin and mix well.

Preheat oven to 350°F (180°C). Spread batter in prepared pan and bake for 14–18 minutes. Immediately loosen cake and invert onto towel.

	icing sugar	

Remove wax paper and sprinkle cake with icing sugar. Roll towel and cake together from narrow end. Cool on wire rack. Unroll.

	Filling:	
1 cup	**powdered sugar**	250 mL
6 oz	**cream cheese**	200 g
½ tsp	**vanilla**	2 mL

Beat sugar, cream cheese and vanilla until smooth. Spread over cake, roll up and chill at least 30 minutes. Slice to serve.

Alternate Filling #1:

1 cup	**whipping cream**	250 mL
¼ cup	**sugar**	50 mL
1 Tbsp	**molasses**	15 mL
½ cup	**cooked pumpkin**	125 mL
½ cup	**flaked coconut**	125 mL

Beat cream, adding sugar. Fold in molasses, pumpkin and coconut. Spread over cake, roll up and chill at least 30 minutes. Slice to serve.

Alternate Filling #2

ice cream to taste

Soften ice cream and spread on cake. Freeze until ready to serve.

Joyce Johnson

Dot Yeatman, Lizzie Law, Grace Yeatman and Mrs. James Ford enjoy tea together at Hyacinthe Bay, Quadra Island, 1915. CRM 4352.

Salmonberries and Muckamuck

The salmonberry is a member of the rose family, but the fruit looks more like a large raspberry, in colours ranging from gold to salmon to deep red. The berries are usually eaten fresh because they have too much water to be dried into fruit leather like raspberries and blackberries. But when they ripen in the early summer—weeks before any other berries are ready—they are welcome indeed. The sprouts of the salmonberry, called muckamuck (also the Chinook jargon word for food), are a traditional spring delicacy among all West Coast aboriginal groups. They are gathered and peeled, then eaten fresh or steamed. Served with a good dinner of salmon, or eaten with sugar as a sweet treat, muckamuck is still one of the coast's favourite foods. Kids love it.

Bruce's Orange Pudding

Serves 6

3	**oranges, peeled and sliced**	3
2 Tbsp	**sugar**	30 mL

Place oranges in a shallow baking dish and sprinkle with sugar.

	Custard:	
3	**egg yolks**	3
2 cups	**milk**	500 mL
¾ cup	**sugar**	175 mL
3 Tbsp	**cornstarch**	45 mL
dash	**salt**	dash

Cook yolks, milk, sugar, cornstarch and salt in a double boiler or on very low heat, stirring constantly until thickened.

1 tsp	**vanilla**	5 mL

Add vanilla and mix well. Pour custard over the oranges.

	Meringue:	
3	**egg whites**	3
6 Tbsp	**sugar**	90 mL

Beat egg whites until stiff, adding sugar gradually.

Preheat oven to 400°F (200°C). Cover custard with meringue and bake until golden brown.

Myra Baikie

Oranges in Red Wine

Serves 6

1 cup	**dry red wine**	250 mL
1 cup	**water**	250 mL
⅓ cup	**honey**	75 mL
2	**cinnamon sticks**	2
4	**cloves**	4
2	**lemon slices**	2

Combine wine, water, honey, cinnamon, cloves and lemon slices. Bring to a boil and simmer 3 minutes. Remove cloves, keep syrup hot.

6	**large oranges**	6
	orange peel	

Peel oranges, reserving skins. Section the oranges, keeping segments as whole as possible. Discard fibrous membrane. Drop orange sections into hot syrup.

   Pare away the white part of the orange peel and cut skin into very fine julienne strips. Sprinkle over the oranges, chill.

1 cup	**whipped cream**	250 mL
	sugar to taste	

Serve with sweetened whipped cream.

Martha James

Smooth Rich Chocolate Pâté

Serves 12
Chill for 4 hours

14 oz	**semi-sweet chocolate, chopped**	400 g

Set a bowl over hot water and melt chocolate. Let cool completely, stirring occasionally. Line an 8x4" (20x10 cm) loaf pan with plastic wrap.

1¾ cups	**whipping cream**	425 mL
1 Tbsp	**liqueur,** your choice	15 mL

In a separate bowl, whip cream and add liqueur. Whisk one quarter of the cream mixture into chocolate. Fold in remaining cream mixture. Spoon into prepared loaf pan and smooth top. Cover and refrigerate for 4 hours or up to 3 days.

	Crème Anglaise:	
2	**egg yolks**	2
⅓ cup	**sugar**	75 mL

Whisk yolks and sugar together in a bowl.

2 cups	**milk**	500 mL
1 tsp	**vanilla**	5 mL

In a saucepan, heat milk just until bubbles form around the edge. Whisk ⅔ cup (150 mL) of the milk into yolk mixture, then return it to the saucepan, stirring constantly. Cook over medium heat for 3–5 minutes or until thickened slightly. *Do not boil.* Strain immediately through a fine sieve to ensure silky consistency.

Stir in vanilla. Place plastic wrap directly on surface. Refrigerate until chilled or up to 1 day.

	Sauce:	
1 cup	**water**	250 mL
½ cup	**sugar**	125 mL
raspberry jam or fresh raspberry pulp to taste		

Make a syrup by boiling water and sugar. Strain the jam or raspberry pulp and add to syrup.

icing sugar

To serve, unmold pâté. Cut into ½" (1 cm) slices and place on dessert plates. Spoon 3 Tbsp (45 mL) Crème Anglaise around each serving. Sprinkle Crème Anglaise with droplets of raspberry sauce. Using a toothpick, swirl raspberry sauce to make attractive pattern. Dust lightly with icing sugar and serve.

Lois Bonning

Apple Meringue Topping

Makes 2½ cups (625 mL)

½ cup	**grated raw apple**	125 mL
½ cup	**sugar**	125 mL
1	**egg white, unbeaten**	1

Grate apple and mix with sugar and egg white immediately to prevent discoloration. Beat all together until mixture is the consistency of whipped cream. Use to top simple desserts or cake. If used as a cake topping, pile mixture lightly on a cold cake that is to be used soon after it is frosted.

British Columbia Women's Institutes
1958 Centennial Cookbook

The Women's Institutes

The Women's Institute is a Canadian organization conceived in 1897 as a means of promoting improved health and homemaking skills among rural women. Numerous groups formed in the North Vancouver Island region during the First World War. The Women's Institute offered isolated women a cherished opportunity for social gatherings, a structure for sharing new ideas and information and a means to accomplish community work. The Apple Topping comes from a province-wide compilation published during the British Columbia Centennial in 1958.

A tennis party at the "Big House" (Pidcock residence), Quathiaski Cove, c. 1912. CRM 11536.

Tart Lemon Mousse with Berry Sauce

Serves 6
Chill 5 hours

Prepare soufflé dish by pinning wax paper collar around edge to extend 2" (5 cm) above rim.

1 pkg	**unflavoured gelatin**	1 pkg
¼ cup	**cold water**	50 mL
¾ cup	**sugar**	175 mL

Combine gelatin and water, let stand 5 minutes. Stir gelatin mixture over low heat until dissolved. Add sugar and cook until dissolved. Remove from heat.

1½ Tbsp	**grated lemon rind**	22 mL
⅔ cup	**fresh lemon juice**	150 mL

Stir lemon rind and juice into gelatin mixture. Set saucepan in water and ice, and stir until almost set. Remove from ice and stir vigorously.

4	**egg whites**	4
⅛ tsp	**salt**	.5 mL
½ cup	**sugar**	125 mL

Beat egg whites and salt to form soft peaks. Beat in sugar, a little at a time, until whites are firm and glossy.

1 cup	**whipping cream**	250 mL

In a separate bowl, whip cream until it forms soft peaks. Fold gelatin mixture thoroughly into egg whites. Gently fold in the whipped cream. Turn the mousse into prepared soufflé dish and chill for 5 hours.

	Sauce:	
2 cups	**fresh strawberries**	500 mL
10 oz	**raspberries, in syrup, thawed**	284 mL
2 Tbsp	**sugar**	30 mL
3½ Tbsp	**kirsch or raspberry liqueur**	52 mL

Set aside 4 strawberries for garnish. Combine the remaining berries and their syrup with the sugar and liqueur, and allow to macerate for 30 minutes. Purée in blender and press through a sieve. Cover and chill.

mint leaves

To serve, cut the 4 saved strawberries lengthwise and press flat sides into the mousse. Use mint leaves to add colour. Pour a few spoonfuls of sauce on each plate, divide mousse among the dessert plates and add another dollop of sauce to each serving.

Judy Price Sturgis

" If we had snow or ice around at Christmas, Mother made ice cream, a lovely boiled custard and cream. The method of freezing was far from modern. Father would bring in a big wooden bucket filled with snow or ice which he'd sprinkle well with salt. Mother put the custard in the snow right to the top and twisted it back and forth in the snow or ice. We used to help but little arms soon tired and Father finished it. We were all served a little dish before we went to bed."

Katie (Walker) Clarke

"I worked for the Union Steamships in 1950. My official position was fourth cook on the M.V. *Chilcotin*. A la modeing pies was the part I liked best as I was an ice cream-a-holic. On certain days the crew was served ice cream, but this day was not one of them.

I was about to empty the large cloth bag from the coffee urn when the ship rolled and I dumped a bucket-sized blob of steaming grounds into an open vat of ice cream.

The normal noisy bedlam in the galley stopped as the chefs and crew stared stunned at this disaster. I instinctively grabbed a large spoon and started digging, racing the hot pellets of coffee as they melted through gallons of succulent ice cream. Just as I was about to scrape out the last of them, I felt a viselike grip on my shoulder as the head chef grabbed me and bellered, 'SMITH! Vot the hell you doing!' A very understandable question as I was head first in the ice cream vat and throwing great globs of coffee and ice cream over my shoulder and onto the galley deck. My urgent and breathless explanation was not acceptable and he ordered me to throw out the last few gallons of ice cream, clean up the mess and get back to work. My love for ice cream overcame my good sense and I chose to argue.

'But sir, there's still a lot of good ice cream left. Here, look, it's just fine,' and I scooped a large speckled spoonful into my mouth and gulped, 'We can't waste it, I'll give it to the crew.' Wrong move.

Continued on page 181

Oma's Cheesecake

Serves 8

Pastry:

¾ cup	**margarine or butter**	175 mL
½ cup	**sugar**	125 mL
2	**egg yolks (reserve whites)**	2

Beat margarine until creamy. Beat in sugar and egg yolks.

2 cups	**flour**	500 mL
2 tsp	**baking powder**	10 mL
1 Tbsp	**milk**	15 mL

Mix flour and baking powder together. Gradually beat into butter mixture. Beat milk in last. The dough will feel like cookie dough.

Beginning with the sides, press dough into a springform pan, about three-quarters the way up. Try to press thinly but enough to make a good wall for the cake. (Using a glass to roll the dough onto the sides works well.) Press remaining dough onto the bottom of the pan. Prick bottom dough lightly with a fork.

	Filling:	
16 oz	**cream cheese**	450 g
4	**egg yolks (reserve whites)**	4

Beat cheese until creamy. Add egg yolks one at a time, mixing until smooth.

pinch	**salt**	pinch
1 cup	**whipping cream**	250 mL
1 tsp	**vanilla**	5 mL

Beat in salt, unwhipped cream and vanilla.

6	**egg whites**	6
½ cup	**sugar**	125 mL

In a separate bowl, beat egg whites to soft peaks, adding sugar. Fold egg whites into cream cheese mixture.

Preheat oven to 325°F (160°C). Pour filling into prepared crust and bake for 45–60 minutes. Cheesecake is done when knife inserted in centre comes out clean.

Leona Perkins

Easy Amaretto Cheesecake

Serves 8
Chill before serving

Crust:

1	**graham wafer pie crust**	1
1	**square semi-sweet chocolate, finely grated**	1

Follow directions on graham wafer package for a 9" (23 cm) pie crust. Sprinkle half of grated chocolate over crust.

Filling:

32	**large marshmallows**	32
½ cup	**milk**	125 mL

In a double boiler, heat marshmallows and milk, stirring constantly until marshmallows are melted. If using microwave, heat 1 minute at a time, then stir. Chill until thickened.

¼ cup	**Amaretto liqueur**	50 mL
2 Tbsp	**brandy**	30 mL

Stir liqueurs into marshmallow mixture.

1 cup	**whipping cream, chilled**	250 mL
8 oz	**cream cheese**	225 g

In a chilled bowl, whip the cream and add cream cheese. Fold this mixture into the marshmallows. Pour over crust. Sprinkle the remaining grated chocolate on top.

Betty Crawford

Head chefs were traditionally big, tough, and short tempered. He grabbed a meat cleaver, pushed his red face into mine and shouted, 'You will throw out ze ice cream NOW!'

I wrapped my arms around the ice cream vat and ran. The chase was on. The chef, with meat cleaver raised, charged, slipping and sliding in the mushy mess on the deck. Around and around the galley we raced until he grabbed me by the back of my pants and threw both me and the ice cream into the dishwashing tubs and turned the hot water on full blast. I was horror-struck as I watched all that delicious ice cream swirl out the drain. The chef left us there to melt and stomped away.

The outcome of all this was, in support of my efforts, the crew went on a 'silent strike' for the rest of the day."

Richard "Mickey" Smith,
CRM aural history

Chocolate Layer Cake with Raspberry Filling

Serves 8
Chill filling 2 hours

Batter:

2 cups	**flour**	500 mL
1½ tsp	**baking soda**	7 mL
¾ tsp	**baking powder**	3 mL
1 tsp	**salt**	5 mL

In a large bowl sift flour, baking soda, baking powder and salt together.

1 cup	**sugar**	250 mL
¼ cup	**butter**	50 mL
2	**large eggs**	2

In another bowl, beat sugar and butter until light and fluffy. Add eggs one at a time, beating each egg in.

4 oz	**unsweetened chocolate**	112 g
1 cup	**sour cream**	250 mL
1 tsp	**vanilla**	5 mL
⅔ cup	**water**	150 mL

Melt chocolate and cool it a bit. Beat chocolate, sour cream, vanilla and water into egg mixture. Then add flour mixture and beat at high speed for 3 minutes. Preheat oven to 350°F (180°C).

Pour batter into two greased 9" (23 cm) cake pans. Bake for 35–40 minutes. Cool in pans for 10 minutes and then flip out onto racks.

Filling:

4 cups	**raspberries, fresh or frozen**	900 mL
1 pkg	**unflavoured gelatin**	1 pkg

Mash raspberries to create a bit of juice. Heat up about half the raspberries. Add gelatin. Cook this mixture, stirring constantly, for 3 minutes. Mix the cooked raspberries and gelatin with the remaining raspberries and chill for 2 hours or more.

Icing:

8 oz	**semisweet chocolate, melted**	225 g
1 cup	**sour cream, at room temp.**	250 mL
pinch	**salt**	pinch
½ tsp	**vanilla**	2 mL

Melt chocolate and cool slightly. Beat together chocolate, sour cream, salt and vanilla. This should be glossy. If the sour cream is too cold the icing will become too firm, in which case beat in 1–2 Tbsp (15–30 mL) hot water to soften. Assemble the layers with filling spread in the middle and frost with icing.

Jeanette Taylor

Peach Beehives

Serves 4

1	**recipe rich pastry (single-crust)**	1

Roll out pastry in a long rectangle. Cut lengthwise into ½" (1 cm) wide strips.

4	**fresh peaches**	4

Wash and dry peaches and remove stem ends. Do not peel. Place peach, stem end down, on counter. Starting at the top, wrap pastry strips around peach, overlapping each row until peach is completely covered.

Preheat oven to 375°F (190°C). Place peaches in a shallow baking pan and bake for 30–40 minutes or until well browned.

Sauce:

2–3 Tbsp	**flour**	30–45 mL
3 Tbsp	**butter, melted**	45 mL
2 cups	**water**	500 g
	sugar and nutmeg to taste	

Add flour to melted butter to make a roux. Add remaining ingredients and cook over low heat until consistency of gravy. Serve hot and pass nutmeg sauce to spoon over peach beehives.

British Columbia Women's Institutes
1958 Centennial Cookbook

Millie's Zucchini-Almond Cake

Serves 10

4	eggs, beaten	4
3 cups	sugar	750 mL
1¼ cups	vegetable oil	300 mL
1 tsp	almond extract	5 mL

Berry cakes were once a favourite of the Kwakwaka'wakw people. Currants, salal berries (yama), raspberries, red elderberries or a mixture of them were steamed or boiled, then placed in cedar frames, spread on racks and dried slowly over a fire. The cakes were tied into bundles and stored in cedar boxes. They were eaten with eulachon grease at feasts, using special black spoons made of mountain goat horn. Red elderberry cakes were never eaten before noon because they were thought to give people stomach aches if eaten in the morning.

In a large bowl, beat eggs until light and thick. Add sugar ½ cup (125 mL) at a time, beating well after each addition. Stir in oil and almond extract.

3 cups	all-purpose flour	750 mL
2 tsp	baking powder	10 mL
1 tsp	baking soda	5 mL
1 tsp	salt	5 mL
1 cup	ground almonds	250 mL

In a separate bowl, combine all dry ingredients.

3 cups	finely grated zucchini	750 mL

Preheat oven to 350°F (180°C).

Add dry ingredients and zucchini to egg mixture, mixing until smooth. Pour into a greased tube pan and bake for 1 hour and 15 minutes. Cool in pan for 15 minutes. Remove cake from pan and cool on rack.

Glaze:		
1¼ cups	icing sugar	300 mL
2 Tbsp	milk	30 mL
¼ tsp	almond extract	1 mL

Mix all icing ingredients together and spread on top of cake, letting it drip down the sides.

	slivered almonds (optional)	

Sprinkle with slivered almonds if desired.

Millie Lloyd

Strawberry Meringue Roll

Serves 8–10

Batter:		
4	**egg yolks**	4
¼ cup	**sugar**	50 mL
¼ tsp	**salt**	1 mL
½ tsp	**vanilla**	2 mL

Beat yolks until thick and lemon coloured. Gradually add sugar, salt and vanilla.

4	**egg whites**	4

In a separate bowl, beat whites until very stiff. Fold in yolk mixture.

¾ cup	**flour**	175 mL
1 tsp	**baking powder**	5 mL

Preheat oven to 375°F (190°C).

Sift dry ingredients together and fold into egg mixture. Line a 10x15"
(25x38 cm) cookie sheet with wax paper and bake for 12 minutes. Turn onto
cloth dusted with icing sugar. Roll quickly, paper inside. Cool on rack.

Filling:		
¾ cup	**whipping cream**	175 mL
2 Tbsp	**sugar**	30 mL
1 cup	**sliced strawberries**	250 mL

Whip cream, adding sugar. Fold strawberries into whipped cream.
Unroll cooled cake. Remove paper and spread with filling. Roll up. Chill.

Strawberry Meringue:		
¾ cup	**sliced strawberries**	175 mL
½ cup	**sugar**	125 mL
1	**egg white**	1
dash	**salt**	dash

Combine all meringue ingredients and beat with electric beater until mixture
is very stiff, about 7–10 minutes. Frost chilled roll with strawberry meringue.

British Columbia Women's Institutes
1958 Centennial Cookbook

Wild Berries

The trailing wild blackberry (*Rubus ursinus*) with its intense flavour grows along gravel roads and on the logging slash. The Himalayan blackberry, with larger fruit growing on tall canes, was introduced and has naturalized in thickets. The many varieties of huckleberries abound, the common red berry (*Vaccinium parvifolium*) on large shrubs at low elevations and the blue huckleberry (*Vaccinium membranaceum*) in the mountains.

Salmonberries (*Rubus spectabilis*) and thimbleberries (*Rubus leucodermis*) are also collected for jams and pies but are not as delicious as other wild berries.

Wild Berry Deep Dish Pie

Serves 6

Sweet Pastry:		
1¼ cups	flour	300 mL
6 Tbsp	butter, frozen	90 mL
2 Tbsp	shortening	30 mL
dash	salt	dash
¼ cup	sugar	50 mL
	ice water	

Process flour, butter, shortening, salt and sugar until consistency of corn-meal. Add ice water slowly, up to 3 Tbsp (45 mL), until the dough begins to form a ball.

Preheat oven to 400°F (200°C). Roll out dough ⅛" (3 mm) thick and place in a pie plate. Bake for 10 minutes.

Filling:		
4 cups	huckleberries and small wild blackberries	900 mL
½ tsp	finely chopped fresh mint	2 mL
4 Tbsp	tapioca	50 mL
1½ cups	sugar, or to taste	375 mL
1¾ cups	ricotta cheese	425 mL
4 Tbsp	Cointreau	50 mL

Crush enough berries to create some juice and add remaining filling ingredients. Pour mixture into the shell. Bake for 40 minutes or until done. Cool to set the pie before serving.

Gerry Coté

Plum Tarts

Serves 12
Chill pastry 1 hour

	Pastry:	
½ cup	**butter, softened**	125 mL
½ cup	**vegetable shortening**	125 mL
⅓ cup	**sugar**	75 mL
2 tsp	**vanilla**	10 mL
2 tsp	**grated lemon rind**	10 mL
2 tsp	**lemon juice**	10 mL
1 tsp	**salt**	5 mL

With electric mixer, cream butter, shortening, sugar, vanilla, lemon rind, lemon juice and salt until light and fluffy.

1	**large egg**	1
1	**large egg yolk**	1

Add whole egg and yolk and continue beating until smooth.

2⅔ cups	**flour**	650 mL

Add flour and stir, then knead to form dough. Wrap and chill for 1 hour. Halve the dough and roll out each half to fit a 17x24" (43x60 cm) cookie sheet with extra on the long edges. Crimp bottom layer up to form an edge.

	Filling:	
¾ cup	**currant jelly, melted**	175 mL
8	**plums, sliced** (different colours are nice)	8

Preheat oven to 375°F (190°C).

Brush each half of rolled dough with ¼ cup (50 mL) of the jelly. Arrange plums overlapping on top. Bake for 30 minutes or until golden. Brush plums with the remaining jelly and cool.

	Topping:	
1 cup	**whipping cream, well chilled**	250 mL
	raspberry brandy to taste	

In a chilled bowl, beat cream with brandy until stiff. Serve the tarts with whipped cream on top.

Jeanette Taylor

Depression Era Coastal Cruising with Amy and Francis Barrow

For those who found satisfaction in a subsistence life, the beautiful collage of islands and inlets between Vancouver Island and the British Columbia mainland provided a bountiful haven during the Depression years. As frequent summer visitors travelling the coast on the *Toketie*, Amy and Francis Barrow captured the spirit and the colourful character of the coast from 1933 to 1941 in film footage, photographs and journals which are now preserved in the Campbell River Museum and the Provincial Archives of British Columbia.

In *Upcoast Summers* Beth Hill describes how the Barrows shared in the life of the coast: "buying vegetables or dairy products from cash-short gardeners, inviting people for meals on the *Toketie* and going happily to dinner in a log cabin, floating fish camp, logging camp, wherever they were invited."

In his journals Francis enthusiastically described Amy's special techniques for preparing their basic live-aboard fare: "July 1, 1935: Very good supper: boiled ling cod, white sauce (made of barley meal, onion, salt, butter), canned peas, cherries, coffee."

Rhubarb was a special favourite of the Barrows, and Francis mentions a number of Amy's favourite concoctions, among them her unique and "delicious" jelly of wild gooseberries, rhubarb and lemon. Not many entries record more than a brief tantalizing mention of their dinners, but Francis did record the recipe for Amy's treasured rhubarb custard pie. It is published here as a very worthy old-fashioned spring treat.

Amy Barrow aboard the Toketie, *c. 1938. In addition to photographs and a journal, Amy's husband Francis recorded their travels by movie camera. He had a particular fondness for filming rapids. CRM 15465.*

Amy Barrow's Rhubarb Pie

Serves 6

1	**pastry shell, unbaked**	1

Your favourite recipe.

	Filling:	
4 cups	**chopped raw rhubarb**	900 g
2 Tbsp	**flour**	30 mL
1 cup	**sugar**	250 mL
¾ tsp	**grated dried ginger**	3 mL

Combine all filling ingredients and place in pie crust.

	Custard:	
3 egg yolks (reserve whites for meringue)		
2 Tbsp	**butter**	30 mL
1 cup	**milk**	250 mL

Preheat oven to 350°F (180°C).
 Beat egg yolks and mix with butter and milk. Pour over filling and bake for 40 minutes until custard is firm.

	Meringue:	
3	**egg whites**	3
¼ cup	**sugar**	50 mL

Beat egg whites until stiff, adding sugar gradually. Spread on top of pie and return to oven until meringue is brown.

Francis Barrow's journal, 1940

"**M**y mother and I used to pick a lot of wild blackberries. We'd take six or eight big pots and come home with them full. Sometimes we'd even have to turn our hats inside out and put some leaves inside and fill our hats too. We canned them and made jam. We'd be in the bush all by ourselves. We'd take a lunch. Mum would cook some new potatoes, some little carrots and some fresh peas from the garden and mix these with lettuce, mayonnaise and green onions, and we'd have an inch of salad between our two pieces of bread. And Boy! Was that good! We drank water off the creek."

Jean (Schibler) Turner, remembering her childhood on the West Coast during the 1920s, CRM aural history

Grand Marnier Parfait

Serves 8–10

Freeze 30 minutes

6 Tbsp	**Grand Marnier**	90 mL
2 Tbsp	**orange juice**	30 mL
1¼ cups	**almond macaroon or graham wafer crumbs**	300 mL

In a small bowl, mix 3 Tbsp (45 mL) of the Grand Marnier with the orange juice. Add crumbs and set aside.

5	**egg yolks**	5
½ cup	**sugar**	125 mL

In another small bowl beat egg yolks and sugar for 5 minutes, until mixture is very pale and thick.

1 Tbsp	**grated orange rind**	15 mL

Combine orange rind and remaining Grand Marnier and stir into the egg yolk mixture. Set aside.

5	**egg whites**	5
pinch	**salt**	pinch
3 Tbsp	**sugar**	45 mL

In a large bowl beat egg whites and salt until they form soft peaks. Beat in sugar until stiff but not dry.

2 cups	**whipping cream, softly whipped**	500 mL

Add the yolk mixture and the whipped cream to the egg white mixture. Fold until blended.

   To serve, fill individual parfait glasses or wide wine glasses half full of the egg mixture. Sprinkle with half the crumb mixture. Fill with remaining egg mixture and top with remaining crumbs. Do not smooth the surface. Freeze for at least 30 minutes before serving. The parfait keeps up to 4 weeks in the freezer if you cover tightly to make airtight.

Holly Anderson

Hazelnut Torte

Serves 8

4	**eggs**	4
¾ cup	**sugar**	175 mL

Blend eggs and sugar in food processor or blender.

2 Tbsp	**flour**	30 mL
2½ tsp	**baking powder**	12 mL
1 cup	**finely ground hazelnuts**	250 mL

Add flour, baking powder and hazelnuts and blend at high speed.
   Preheat oven to 350°F (180°C). Pour batter into two greased 8" (20 cm) round pans or a greased jelly roll pan. Bake for 20 minutes.

	Frosting:	
½ tsp	**instant coffee**	5 mL
¾ cup	**whipping cream**	175 mL
2 Tbsp	**icing sugar**	30 mL
	vanilla to taste	

Sprinkle instant coffee granules on top of cream and beat until stiff. Stir in icing sugar and vanilla to taste.

	raspberry jam	

To assemble: Cut cake into two halves if baked in a jelly roll pan. Spread a little raspberry jam on bottom layer, then a little whipped cream on top of jam. Place top layer on cake. Frost cake with remaining whipped cream.

Mary Bennett

A refreshing dip on a summer's day.
Swimming lessons at the Tyee Spit,
Campbell River, 1950s.
CRM 2837

COOKIES &
BARS

Thin Oat Cookies

Makes about 6 dozen

1 cup	**margarine**	250 mL
1 cup	**brown sugar**	250 mL
½ cup	**white sugar**	125 mL
1	**egg**	1

Cream margarine and sugar until fluffy. Add egg, mix well.

1½ cups	**flour**	375 mL
1 tsp	**baking powder**	5 mL
½ tsp	**salt**	2 mL
1 tsp	**baking soda**	5 mL

Add flour, baking powder, salt and soda and mix well.

1¼ cups	**oatmeal**	300 mL
¾ cup	**coconut**	175 mL

Add oatmeal and coconut, mix all together. Preheat oven to 375°F (190°C). Drop dough by spoonfuls onto greased cookie sheets and press with a fork. Dip fork in flour so it doesn't stick to the dough, and press fairly flat so they will be crisp. Bake until lightly browned.

Dora McCallum

Catherine Green Tuck grew up on Quadra Island during the 1930s and '40s, and she remembers afternoon tea rituals that included light cookies like these.

"When we were little girls growing up in our Victorian mother's household at Quathiaski Cove, the serving of afternoon tea to a few invited guests was a very special and respected event. Sandwiches were made with thinly sliced bread and the crusts were cut off, not like school sandwiches. There might be a layer cake with raspberry filling and powdered sugar on top, and the oatmeal cookies were pressed especially thin, or even sliced. It was Mother's chance to use her Minton cups and saucers, and the cream and sugar that went with them, her cutwork embroidery linen tea cloth— chastely white, and a black drop-leaf table if she was serving tea indoors."

Catherine Greene Tuck

Graham Wafer Almond Squares

Makes 24 squares

24	**graham wafers**	24

Line a cookie sheet with tinfoil and place 24 wafers close together on foil.

1 cup	**butter**	250 mL
¾ cup	**brown sugar**	175 mL
1 cup	**slivered almonds**	250 mL

Preheat oven to 350°F (180°C).
Bring butter and brown sugar to a boil. Add almonds and spoon the mixture over the graham wafers. Bake for 8 minutes. Cool and slice.

Betty Cunning

A Quadra Island picnic at Cape Mudge Lighthouse, 1903, from Rob Yeatman's photo album. CRM 6133.

Picnicking was a favourite Victorian pastime, and one which was especially cherished by settlers in isolated communities where the time and occasion to gather together were rare. The late Katie (Walker) Clarke came to Quadra as a child in 1893. She remembered the first community picnic held in honour of Queen Victoria's Diamond Jubilee in 1897. "All the neighbours and friends gathered at Cape Mudge to honour the Queen. The Pidcocks took all the Cove people and those living near on their tug, the *Quathiaski*. A large table cloth, or a number of them, were spread under the trees. The children raced around like wild things getting acquainted, especially the three Walkers. Such a spread of good food. Mrs. Bryant had fattened and cooked a delicious suckling pig, apple in its mouth too, in spite of it being June. Mrs. Emma Yeatman had a chicken pie made in a milk pan. The Pidcocks brought oranges, candies and cookies from their store. Our mother was very proud of her green gooseberry pies, the first of the season. Mrs. Joyce had brought several delicious roast chickens. All these were enough to excite us to the highest pitch, besides salads, jellies, cakes and many other kinds of pies."

Katie (Walker) Clarke

Mocha Coffee Bars

Makes 48 bars

1 cup	**butter**	250 mL
1 cup	**brown sugar, packed**	250 mL

Cream butter, add sugar and beat until light.

1	**egg yolk, large**	1
1½ tsp	**vanilla**	7 mL
2 Tbsp	**strong coffee**	30 mL

Beat in yolk and vanilla. Add coffee a little at a time, beating until well combined.

½ tsp	**salt**	2 mL
2 cups	**flour**	500 mL

Add salt and flour and beat well.
Preheat oven to 350°F (180°C). Spread dough evenly in 15½"x10½" (39x27 cm) jelly roll pan and bake for 15–20 minutes.

	Topping:	
8 oz	**semi-sweet chocolate, melted**	225 g
¾ cup	**coarsely chopped pecans**	175 mL

Spread chocolate evenly over baked layer. Sprinkle pecans on top. Let cool in pan. Cut into 48 bars and chill for 15–20 minutes.

Jeanette Taylor

Lemon Squares

Makes one 8x8" (20x20 cm) pan

Crust:		
1 cup	**flour**	250 mL
½ cup	**butter or margarine**	125 mL
¼ cup	**icing sugar**	50 mL

Preheat oven to 350°F (180°C).

Mix all crust ingredients together and pat into a greased 8x8" (20x20 cm) pan. Bake for 15–20 minutes until lightly browned.

Filling:		
2	**eggs**	2
1 cup	**sugar**	250 mL
½ tsp	**baking powder**	2 mL
	grated rind of 1 lemon	
3 Tbsp	**lemon juice**	45 mL
½ tsp	**salt**	2 mL

Beat all ingredients together and pour over crust. Return to the oven for 15–20 minutes until lightly browned and set.

Shirley Hollinger

"The Willows Hotel, beautifully situated on the Valdez Straits within a few yards of the sea, is all that a sportsman could desire. Clean, well-furnished bedrooms, a bathroom and quite a decent table, all for the moderate sum of two dollars a day.

The proprietor did not quite realize the fact that the majority of the guests came for the fishing, and not for the food.

In those glorious autumn evenings, the manageress forgot that a keen fisherman might stay out till nine or even ten, if the fish were taking. Dinner he could not expect, but a cold supper if ordered beforehand, might have been laid out in the dining room.

By making love to the manageress and the Chinese cook, I generally succeeded in finding something to eat if I was late, but I often had to forage for myself in the kitchen."

Sir John Rogers,
Sport in Vancouver and Newfoundland, 1912

Anything Goes Cookies

Makes about 5 dozen

1 cup	**margarine or butter**	250 mL
1 cup	**brown sugar**	250 mL

Cream butter and sugar together.

1 tsp	**baking soda**	5 mL
¼ cup	**hot water**	50 mL

In a separate bowl add baking soda to hot water, then add bubbling liquid to butter and sugar and mix well.

2 cups	**flour**	500 mL
2 cups	**quick rolled oats**	500 mL
10 oz	**chocolate chips**	300 g
½ cup	**shredded coconut**	125 mL
1 cup	**raisins, walnuts, almonds or whatever you have**	250 mL

Mix all dry ingredients, nuts and raisins. Add to butter mixture and mix well. If dough is too dry just add a smidgen of hot water.
Preheat oven to 350°F (180°C). For each cookie, take about a tablespoon of dough, roll between hands and flatten onto cookie sheet. Bake for 8–10 minutes.

Joan Whitmore

"Six of us girls came up in April 1918 to work in the International Timber dining room. My mother didn't want us to come—going out into the logging camp with all the wild men. She thought it would be a rough place. The men weren't very keen about having women in the camp, either.

We were interviewed in Vancouver by the superintendent and his wife. We were to be waitresses. They wanted older girls. Annie Green was thirty-five, Flo was twenty-nine and I was eighteen.

The first thing we had to do was clean the dining room. It was so dirty. We were scrubbing tables and benches, and Spoolie, the locomotive engineer, saw what we were doing. He said, 'How will it be if I back up the engine and hook up the steam hose? That will do the trick.'

We steamed the place. You could see the colour of the wood then. We were treated with all respect."

Gertie Kusha, *CRM aural history. In 1918, Gertie Kusha came to work for International Timber. She married another IT employee, "Spoolie" Kusha, in 1920.*

Buttertart Square

Makes one 9x9" (23x23 cm) pan

Crust:		
1½ cups	**flour**	375 mL
½ cup	**butter**	125 mL
2 Tbsp	**sugar**	30 mL

Preheat oven to 350°F (180°C).

Combine crust ingredients and press into a 9x9" (23x23 cm) pan. Bake for 10 minutes, cool 10 minutes.

Filling:		
2	**eggs**	2
1½ cups	**brown sugar**	375 mL
¼ cup	**melted butter**	50 mL
1 Tbsp	**vinegar**	15 mL
1 tsp	**flour**	5 mL
1 cup	**raisins**	250 mL

Combine all filling ingredients and pour over crust. Bake for 20–25 minutes.

Jackie MacNaughton

It was out on a haywire homeguard
　show
Where the ground was rough and
　the crew was slow;
Where a rusty, crooked railroad
　track
Wound out of camp past the
　rigger's shack.
Within that shack, in wedded bond,
Resided the rigger's wife—a
　blonde—
Who was wont to wave with a glint
　in her eye
At the engineer as he thundered by.
His ancient Climax, worn with years,
Would clash and clang its hypoid
　gears,
Shiver and shake and hump its back
As it wheeled those cars up the
　crooked track.

Robert Swanson,
from "Climax Courageous"

Women were a rare sight in old-time logging camps. Here an all-male crew poses on their Climax locomotive. UBC photo.

Danish Apple Bar

Makes one 12x17" (30x43 cm) pan

	Crust:	
2½ cups	**flour**	625 mL
1 tsp	**salt**	5 mL
1 cup	**shortening or margarine**	250 mL
	1 egg yolk (reserve white) plus enough milk to make ⅔ cup (150 mL) liquid	

Sift flour and salt and cut in shortening until crumbly. Slowly add egg and milk mixture. Lightly stir to moisten. Divide in half and roll out one half to fit 12x17" (30x43 cm) rectangular pan or cookie sheet with sides.

	Filling:	
1 cup	**crushed corn flakes**	250 mL

Sprinkle bottom crust with corn flakes. Do not omit cornflakes, as this acts as a tasty sponge to soak up any apple juices.

4	**cooking apples, peeled**	4
	sugar to taste	
1 tsp	**cinnamon**	5 mL

Slice apples thinly over corn flakes. Sprinkle with sugar and cinnamon. Roll out remaining pastry, cover apples and pinch edges closed.
Preheat oven to 400°F (200°C).

	Topping:	
1	**egg white**	1

Beat egg white until stiff and brush the top crust with it. Bake for 35–40 minutes or until done.

	Icing:	
½ cup	**icing sugar**	125 mL
1 Tbsp	**water**	15 mL
1 tsp	**vanilla**	5 mL

Mix all icing ingredients together to make very runny icing. Drizzle icing over the apple bar while still hot. Serve warm or cold.

Millie Lloyd

Marvellous Marshmallows

Makes one 12x17" (30x43 cm) pan
Chill 30 minutes

2 cups	**sugar**	500 mL
½ cup	**water**	125 mL

Boil sugar and water together for 2 minutes.

2 Tbsp	**gelatin**	30 mL
½ cup	**cold water**	125 mL
1 tsp	**vanilla**	5 mL

Combine gelatin and water to soften. Combine syrup, gelatin mixture and vanilla. Beat with electric mixer until very thick (takes a while). Pour into greased 9x9" (23x23 cm) pan. Cool in refrigerator for 30 minutes or until set.

toasted coconut

Cut marshmallows into squares and roll in toasted coconut.

Martha James

July 1st tug-of-war, Ocean Falls, BC, 1919.

Masquerades added merriment to social events.
Brown & Kirkland Logging crew and their families,
Elk Bay, BC, 1920s.
CRM 14039

HOLIDAY FARE

Memories of Christmas Past

"On Christmas morning, of course, Santa had left us each a gift and a red mesh stocking filled with goodies such as a puzzle, balloon, a book and maybe crayons.

That morning after all the chores were done, we all left in the horse and buggy to join Granny and Grandpa Joyce, their family and friends for a huge dinner at noon. There would often be as many as thirty people at those dinners, including the bachelor fishermen who lived in shacks below the farm.

They must have prepared for weeks—a long table set in the dining room was laden with chickens, turkey, ham, loads of vegetables, yummy dressing and gravy, and for dessert mince pies, tarts and a large plum pudding.

Then if you still felt hungry, there were nuts [which had been gathered from their walnut trees and dried by the stove for holiday baking and eating], candy and Japanese oranges. The oranges could only be bought at Christmas time those days and were a great treat themselves.

In the afternoon we played games, visited until a cold supper—as sumptuous as the dinner—was served. After clean-up, to the living room with its fireplace blazing, with a Christmas tree with presents for all and, of course, a jolly Santa."

Eve (Willson) Eade,
CRM aural history

"Around 1927, on Christmas we'd often have a goose dinner. My mum would pluck them and save the feathers for a quilt. Or we'd have roast pork. Dad would kill a pig. We'd also have potatoes and gravy and salad. We had everything canned. Mum had a big, big garden she worked on all year and she'd have five or six hundred jars put away for every winter ... vegetables, fruit, jam, meat, fish. We had lots to eat; potatoes, carrots, parsnips, turnips and beets were in the root house. We had one hundred fruit trees in the orchard, cherries, plums and apples. Among the apples we had 'keepers' that lasted until spring. We had six acres, fairly much cleared."

Jean (Schibler) Turner,
CRM aural history

Festive Seafood Casserole

Serves 4–6

	Sauce:	
4 Tbsp	**butter**	50 mL
4 Tbsp	**flour**	50 mL
	salt and pepper to taste	
1¾ cups	**light cream**	425 mL
2 Tbsp	**dry sherry**	30 mL

Make a roux of butter and flour, add salt and pepper and cream, stirring constantly to sauce consistency. Add sherry.

1 cup	**cooked halibut**	250 mL
1 cup	**cooked prawns**	250 mL
2 Tbsp	**butter**	30 mL
1 Tbsp	**chopped shallots**	15 mL
2 lbs	**chanterelles**	900 g

Use whatever seafood combinations you like. Combine sauce and remaining ingredients in a casserole.

buttered bread crumbs
parmesan cheese

Preheat oven to 350°F (180°C).
Top casserole with buttered bread crumbs and parmesan cheese. Bake for 30 minutes.

Mary Bennett

In 1791 a crew from the American fur-trading ship *Columbia* spent the winter ashore near Tofino and celebrated Christmas. Captain Robert Gray invited many Natives to join his crew in the festivities. Decorations included branches of cedar and Oregon grape. The dinner was a gigantic barbecue. Around the fire in three tiers, twenty geese were roasted and nearby, on a spit, was a side of venison.

"Each Christmas Granny [Anna Joyce] would invite the returned soldiers (1914–18) up for Christmas dinner and give them a present of her Christmas cakes baked in coffee tins."

Gladys Knappett

Free Press Dollar Fruit Cake

Serves 10

1 cup	**butter**	250 mL
1 cup	**sugar**	250 mL
3	**eggs, well beaten**	3

Cream butter until very light, add sugar gradually and continue creaming until mixture is very fluffy and almost colourless. Add eggs and mix in thoroughly.

2 cups	**sultana raisins**	500 mL
½ cup	**chopped walnuts**	125 mL
½ cup	**blanched and chopped almonds**	125 mL
2 cups	**mixed peel**	500 mL
8 oz	**glazed cherries, chopped**	225 g

Wash raisins by pouring boiling water over them, and dry them thoroughly between towels. Place raisins in a bowl with the walnuts, almonds, peel and cherries.

2 cups	**flour**	500 mL
1 tsp	**baking powder**	5 mL
¼ tsp	**salt**	1 mL
¼ cup	**fruit juice**	50 mL
1 tsp	**brandy**	5 mL

Sift flour, baking powder and salt over fruit. Mix well.

   Preheat oven to 300°F (150°C). Add the floured fruit to the egg mixture with the fruit juice and brandy. Line a tube pan with 2 layers of greased brown paper. Bake cake for 2 hours on lower rack.

Dora McCallum

Mincemeat

Makes about 6 lbs (2.7 kg)

1 lb	**suet**	450 g
1 lb	**raisins**	450 g
1 lb	**currants**	450 g
2 lbs	**sugar**	900 g
juice and grated rind of 3 lemons		
1 lb	**apples, chopped**	450 g
2 oz	**mixed peel**	60 g
½ cup	**chopped almonds**	125 mL
3 tsp	**marmalade**	15 mL
1 cup	**brandy**	250 mL

Mix all ingredients together. Store in refrigerator.

June Painter

"At Christmas time the logging camps would shut down and most men would go home or to Vancouver. Some stayed around Campbell River and the Thulins put on special Christmas spreads for them at the Willows Hotel. The family still have two menus printed for the Christmas of 1910 and among the fare is listed: stewed beef tomatoes, mutton chops, cold sugar cured ham, head cheese, tapioca pudding with lemon sauce and plum pie.

There was a memorable Christmas in Holberg when the barge that brought the turkeys and other groceries from Vancouver could not land in Holberg because the inlet was frozen. Hot dogs were on the Christmas menu that week."

Upper Islander,
December 22, 1982

The Ellison party at Willows Hotel, Campbell River, 1910. The Honourable Price Ellison, Minister of Public Works, headed an expedition to explore the potential of the area, which became Strathcona Park, BC's first provincial park, in 1911. CRM 10089.

Granny's Christmas Pudding

Serves 20

Steam 5 hours

	juice and grated rind of 2 lemons	
1 lb	currants	450 g
1 lb	raisins	450 g
1 lb	sugar	450 g
1 lb	suet	450 g
1 lb	bread crumbs (no crusts)	450 g
8 oz	almonds	225 g
1 lb	flour	450 g
2	carrots, grated	2
6	eggs, well beaten	6
1 tsp	salt	5 mL
1 tsp	baking soda	5 mL
1 tsp	nutmeg	5 mL
1 tsp	cinnamon	5 mL
1 tsp	vanilla	5 mL
½ cup	brandy	125 mL

Pour juice and rind of lemons over the currants and raisins and let soak.
Grease a mold large enough to hold pudding. Mix all ingredients together and
fill mold two-thirds full, cover with oiled lid and steam 5 hours.

June Painter

Fruit Cake Cookies

Makes about 6 dozen

1 cup	**raisins**	250 mL
1 cup	**candied pineapple, coarsely chopped**	250 mL
1 cup	**candied cherries, coarsely chopped**	250 mL
1 cup	**brazil nuts, coarsely chopped**	250 mL

Combine fruit and nuts.

½ cup	**golden shortening**	125 mL
¾ cup	**sugar**	175 mL
1	**egg**	1
1 tsp	**vanilla**	5 mL
½ tsp	**almond extract**	2 mL

With an electric mixer, cream shortening, sugar, eggs, vanilla and almond extract on medium speed.

1¼ cups	**flour**	300 mL
½ tsp	**baking soda**	2 mL

Preheat oven to 350°F (180°C).
Combine dry ingredients and add to creamed mixture. Fold in fruits and nuts.
Drop by heaping spoonfuls on greased cookie sheet. Bake for 12 minutes.

Anne Saunders

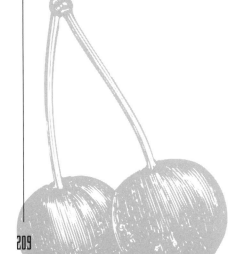

Hamilton's Cranberry Farm, Campbell River

A few locals pick the wild bog cranberries (*Vaccinium oxycoccus*) or the high bush type, but most of us rely on commercial growers. The Hamilton family, father George and sons Neil and Geoff, decided to plant cranberries on their somewhat wet land in 1980. In 1992, they harvested one million pounds from their 60-acre cranberry farm on York Road. The Hamiltons are contracted to the Ocean Spray Co-operative and all their berries are trucked to Richmond, BC for processing.

Ask any kindergarten child where the farm is; most have had a tour there in late September to see the harvesting. The family generously sets aside two weeks for children's tours at this time.

Cranberry Rum Sauce

Makes 2 cups (500 mL)

2 cups	**fresh cranberries**	500 mL
½ cup	**pineapple juice**	125 mL
¾ cup	**sugar**	175 mL
1 tsp	**shredded orange peel**	5 mL
¼ tsp	**shredded lemon peel**	1 mL

Combine first five ingredients and bring to a boil; simmer 10 minutes or until cranberries are tender.

¼ cup	**rum**	50 mL
2 Tbsp	**butter**	30 mL
dash	**salt**	dash

Add remaining ingredients and stir well. Serve over puddings, cakes or ice cream.

Beth Hamilton

Frosted Cranberry Cardamom Munchies

Makes 4 cups (900 mL)

4 cups	**fresh cranberries**	900 mL
1	**egg white, beaten**	1

Coat cranberries in egg white.

1½ cups	**sugar**	375 mL
1 tsp	**ground cardamom**	5 mL

Combine sugar and cardamom and toss cranberries in a few at a time. Place on cookie sheet and let dry at room temperature. Store in airtight container at room temperature for up to 3 weeks.

Beth Hamilton

Cranberry Pear Pie

Serves 6

1	recipe pastry (two-crust)	1

Prepare your favourite pastry recipe for a 9" (23 cm) pie.

	Filling:	
3 cups	fresh cranberries	700 mL
1 cup	water	250 mL

Bring cranberries and water to a boil and simmer 4 minutes.

1½ cups	sugar	375 mL
¼ cup	cornstarch	50 mL
¼ tsp	cinnamon	1 mL

Mix sugar, cornstarch and cinnamon together and add to cranberries. Continue cooking and stirring until mixture thickens. Remove from heat.

2 cups	sliced fresh pears	500 mL

Gently stir in pears. Preheat oven to 400°F (200°C).

Roll out one pie crust and place in pie shell. Fill the pie and add a lattice work of pastry on top. Bake for 40 minutes.

Beth Hamilton

"**O**ur neighbours had goats and a Billy goat smelled fierce when the wind blew towards our house. They raised turkeys too, and one very poor Christmas one of my sisters decided we would have a turkey dinner, poor or not. So she took a couple of handfuls of grain over to the dividing fence and coaxed one of the turkeys to follow her to our barn where she planned this quick end—chopped off his head. The neighbours never did say that they were missing one bird."

Eve (Willson) Eade,
from memoirs at CRM archives

"When Wallace and I went to Vancouver Jim [Robson] picked us up from the CPR boat at Pier D with his big new Cadillac. We spent all morning touring the mill and looking over the yard where the timbers were stacked ready to be shipped by rail car. At lunchtime he took us over to the Westminster Club. The steward brought a bottle of Scotch out of his locker. After the glasses and ice were brought, he poured us each a drink then promptly put the cork back in and placed the bottle on the floor by his side. This action seemed a bit strange to us until he explained. In 1946 he was in the club having a drink when a big earthquake struck. In the confusion his bottle fell off the table and broke. He lost all his Scotch and he was not taking any more chances. That is what we termed being very careful."

Harper Baikie,
A Boy and His Axe

Banana Punch

Serves 20
Freeze overnight

	Syrup:	
4 cups	**water**	900 mL
¼ cup	**sugar**	50 mL

Boil water and sugar together for 5 minutes.

5	**bananas**	5
42 oz	**pineapple juice**	1.5 L
6 oz	**orange juice concentrate**	200 mL
6 oz	**lemonade concentrate**	200 mL

Blend bananas in blender and mix with fruit juices. Add to syrup and freeze overnight.

2 qts	**ginger ale**	2 L

Take fruit mixture out of freezer 4 hours before serving and add ginger ale.

3 cups	**vodka or champagne** (optional)	750 mL

To spike it up, mix in vodka or champagne to taste.

Judy Price Sturgis

Citrus Cooler

Makes 6 pints (1.5 L)
Let stand overnight

2 oz	**citric acid** (available at pharmacy)	60 g
6–8 cups	**sugar**	1.5–2 L
8 cups	**boiling water**	2 L

Combine citric acid and sugar. Pour boiling water over and stir until dissolved.

juice and grated rind of 6 oranges
juice of 2 lemons

Add fruit juices and rind. Let stand overnight, strain and bottle.
To serve, pour ¼ cup (50 mL) of the concentrate in a large glass and add cold water and ice.

Margaret Emma Anderson

Our Mulled Wine

Makes 6 qts (6 L)
Prepare several hours ahead

1	**orange**	1
1	**lemon**	1
3 qts	**dry red wine**	3 L
6 cups	**apple juice**	1.4 L
6 cups	**pineapple juice**	1.4 L
2 cups	**cranberry juice**	500 mL
½ cup	**brown sugar**	125 mL
½	**cinnamon stick**	½

Cut orange and lemon into thin slices. Add remaining ingredients and mix together the morning of the event.
Heat 1½ hours before serving.

Campbell River Museum

"Dad used to make wine in the fall after the frost had been on the parsnips. One summer he decided to make plum wine too as we had lots of plum trees in the orchards and lots of plums after the preserves and jams were made.

One hot summer day my younger sister and I were home alone and we decided to try the wine Dad made. He always said it was so good, so we took the bottle out on the porch and sat and had a few glasses each. It was pretty tasty but when we got up to go into the house, the whole house went round and the rocking chair kept coming for me. We finally crawled to the bed and slept that one off."

Eve (Willson) Eade,
from memoirs at CRM archives

"My dad worked on the railroad when they were putting the branch line through the Okanagan Valley and he was working eighteen hours a day. Christmas didn't mean a thing to him. I could hear my mother crying around Christmas time but I didn't know why. My brother and I wanted to get a Christmas tree but there were no decorations. Mum had saved the silver paper off the tea and the green paper off the Goblin soap. We made tree decorations. My brother and I were too small to chop a tree down but we took the hatchet and went out into the snow bank and got a branch. And that was going to be our Christmas tree.

When Christmas morning came, Dad got up first and he was mad. He woke us up with his swearing and cussing in the kitchen.

'Why don't you clean this place up?' he yelled at my mother, 'I can't get near the stove to light it.'

Well, there were packages everywhere. There was everything anyone could wish for was there. Everything my brother and I wanted was there too. My grandmother and aunt had been into the stores and come back late at night with the stuff. My dad couldn't see Christmas. He just worked."

Flora Brendeland,
CRM aural history

Strawberry Fruit Punch

Serves 20
Chill before serving

Syrup:		
4 cups	**water**	900 mL
4 cups	**sugar**	900 mL

Boil water and sugar for 5 minutes. Chill syrup.

2 qts	**strawberries, hulled**	2 L
1 cup	**sliced pineapple, canned or fresh**	250 mL
3	**bananas, sliced**	3
1 cup	**mixed fruit juice (pineapple, apricot, raspberry)**	250 mL
	juice of 5 large oranges	
	juice of 5 large lemons	

Combine fruit and fruit juices. Add the syrup and chill.

2 qts	**carbonated water**	2 L
3 cups	**crushed ice**	700 mL

Before serving, add carbonated water and crushed ice. This is a strong punch. It is purposely made this way, as the ice will thin it. Water may be added as well, if desired.

Campbell River Museum

The following museum volunteers and other members of the community, past and present, contributed to the realization of this book:

Nikki Adams
Holly Anderson
Joyce Anderson
Margaret E. Anderson
Sherry Anderson
BC Women's Institutes
 1958
Adaline Baikie
Myra Baikie
Ruth Barnett
Amy Barrow
Joyce Bennett
Mary Bennett
Shara Berger
Heather Blackburn
Lois Bonning
Myrna Boulding
Carol Brown
Joan Bunting
Gloria Cameron
Larry Chen
Eleanor Cliffe
Buck Clutterbuck
Don Corker
Gerry Coté
Betty Crawford
Betty Cunning
Vera de Haas
Gerrie Dinsley
Quentin Dodd
Judy Duncan
Betsy Foort
Ian Forbes
Velma Anderson
 Forrester
Bob and Jacquie
 Gordon
Terry Hale
Beth Hamilton

Brenda Hancock
Bill Harrison
Bill Henderson
Annette Hinch
Shirley Hollinger
Betty Hoover
Ermie Iaci
Estelle Inman
Martha James
Vicki Jensen
Joyce Johnson
Anna Joyce
Katherine Knappett
Ross Kondo
Doris Korsa
Richard Krentz
Diana Kretz
Millie Lloyd
Pat Luoma
Rod Macaulay
Dora McCallum
Margo McLoughlin
Jackie MacNaughton
Jessica Madsen
Phil and Margaret
 Margetts
Liz Marti
Iris Martin
Susan Mayse
Win Mayse
Bunny Metcalfe
Brad Mielke
Jacque Mielke
Gladys Mooney
Mike Morin
Margaret Morris
Heather Gordon
 Murphy
Eileen Odowichuk

Morgan Ostler
June Painter
Madge Painter
Katia Panziera
Leona Perkins
Mavis Pickett
Dolly Pidcock
Fran Preston
Daisy Price
Amy Quatell
Dot Quine
Jeanne Ralston
Norma Forrester Rees
Joan Richards
Hope Ross
Irene Ross
Radienber Sangha
Bruce and Anne
 Saunders
Thelma Silkens
Betty Schmidt
Faye Skuse
Jean Stevens
Jay Stewart
Nettie Stewart
Judy Price Sturgis
Audrey Sylvester
Amalia Tancon
Jeanette Taylor
Leona Taylor
Stephanie Tipple
Mary Vogel
June Wagner
June Weatherstone
Joan Whitmore
Margaret Forrester
 Yorke

Potlucks are a tradition with the Museum at Campbell River. Whenever volunteers and staff get together, a fabulous feast instantly materializes. It seems we all share boundless enthusiasm for things edible, along with our common interest in our museum.

Often the museum volunteers and staff see each other only in passing, if at all. Many years ago we began meeting socially over potluck lunches in each other's homes. Legends quickly grew about mouth-watering appetizers, imaginative salads and irresistible desserts. The culinary inspiration then spread to other museum events: members' nights, annual general meetings, VIP receptions, fund-raisers, celebrations. Constant requests for especially popular recipes prompted us to say, "We should do a cookbook."

Producing a cookbook is no simple matter. Between the initial collection of recipes and this finished product an incredible number of hours were dedicated to the project. To achieve balance and representation, we invited others in the community to offer favourite recipes; rigorous testing and selection followed. Oh, the testing! Family, friends and even guest speakers for the museum lecture series were presented with "test dishes" at every opportunity. The potluck linches became organized affairs with assigned recipes subjected to careful evaluation. Then the concept grew to include "a dash of history"—morsels from the museum's archives in quotations, photographs and old-time recipes. Material was compiled, checked, revised, checked, re-revised and checked yet again. By this time an overtaxed computer was demanding retirement.

The Museum at Campbell River, 470 Island Highway, Campbell River, BC. Photo by Dane Simoes.

While the cookbook project was under way, great changes occurred at the Campbell River Museum. Long and intensive effort by trustees, staff, volunteers and members resulted at last in a new facility to accommodate the needs of our busy, constantly growing museum. The spacious new building, on several acres of parkland overlooking Discovery Passage, is home to an impressive artifact collection, an extensive archives and a fine Museum Shop. Work continues on installation of the permanent exhibits while visitors enjoy temporary exhibits and lively, varied programs.

When our beautiful new building was officially opened in February 1994, it was fitting and hardly surprising that volunteers produced a sumptuous array of refreshments for over a thousand visitors and guests.

We hope this book provides not only cooking adventure and enjoyment, but a sense of location and history as well. Ours is a special place with a flavour all its own, and we are happy to share it with you.

Cookbook Committee, The Museum at Campbell River

PAGE	SOURCE
12–13	CRM aural history tape, uncatalogued
15	CRM aural history tape A52-1
16	CRM Archives, vertical file, "Joyce"
17	*Narrative of the Adventures and Sufferings of John R. Jewitt* (London: T. Tegg, 1820)
21	CRM aural history tape A42-1
23	Martin Allerdale Grainger, *Woodsmen of the West* (Toronto: McClelland and Stewart, 1964)
24	Howard White and Jim Spilsbury, *Spilsbury's Coast* (Madeira Park BC: Harbour,1987)
28	CRM aural history tape A49-1
30	*North Island Gazette*, April 1, 1971, article by Neville Shanks
34	CRM aural history tape A138
35	David Ellis and Luke Swan, *Teachings of the Tides* (Penticton: Theytus Books, 1981)
38	Victoria *Times-Colonist*, March 22, 1992
40	CRM aural history tape A29-1
42	CRM aural history tape A164
48	CRM aural history tape A188
49	CRM aural history tape A169
53	CRM aural history tape A23-1
54	CRM Archives, vertical file "Joyce"
56	Journal of BC Exploratory Survey Trip into the Buttle's Lake Region by H. McC. Johnson, 1910, BCARS Add. MSS 249, Vol. 2, file 35
57	B. Guild Gillespie, *On Stormy Seas: The Triumphs and Torments of Captain George Vancouver*, ed. W. Kaye Lamb (Victoria: Horsdal & Schubart, 1992)
61	CRM Archives, vertical file
65	CRM Archives
68	CRM aural history tape A188
69	Capt. James Cook, *A Voyage to the Pacific Ocean 1776-1778*, Vol. II (London: H. Hughs)
70	CRM aural history tape A66-1
71	*Guests Never Leave Hungry: The Autobiography of James Sewid, a Kwakiutl Indian*, ed. James Spradley (Montreal: McGill-Queens University Press, 1972)
75	Ezra Meeker, *Pioneer Reminiscences of Puget Sound* (Lowman & Hanford, 1905)
76	CRM aural history tape A68-1
82	CRM aural history tape A64-2
83	Clellan S. Ford, *Smoke From Their Fires: The Life of a Kwakiutl Chief* (New Haven CT: Yale University Press, 1941)
85	W. Kaye Lamb, ed., *The Voyage of George Vancouver, 1791-1795* (London: Hakluyt Society, 1984)
86	Capt. James Cook, *A Voyage to the Pacific Ocean 1776-1778*, Vol. II (London: H. Hughs)
89	Lewis J. Clark, *Wild Flowers of British Columbia* (Sidney BC: Gray's Publishing, 1973)
101	CRM aural history tape A29-1
107	Top: CRM aural history tape A138; Bottom: CRM aural history tape A48-1
109–10	Leonard Ham, *A Preliminary Survey of Nimpkish Heritage Sites*, Heritage Conservation Branch, October 1980, U'mista oral history tapes HK:1 and TH:5
111	CRM aural history tape A138
112	CRM aural history tape A54
113	CRM aural history tape A138
115	A. V. Ayyar et al, *James Strange's Journal and Narrative of the Commercial Expedition from Bombay to the Northwest Coast of America* (Fairfield WA: Ye Galleon Press, 1982)
116	CRM aural history tape A45-1
117	*Musings*, Vol. VII, No. 3 (November 1988)
119	Florence Tickner, *Fish Hooks and Caulk Boots* (Madeira Park BC: Harbour, 1992)
120	Roderick Haig-Brown, *A River Never Sleeps* (Toronto: Collins, 1974)
121	CRM aural history tape A180
122	Raymond Sokolov, *Fading Feast* (New York: Farrar Straus, 1979)
123	CRM aural history tape A138

PAGE	SOURCE
124	A. V. Ayyar et al, *James Strange's Journal and Narrative of the Commercial Expedition from Bombay to the Northwest Coast of America* (Fairfield WA: Ye Galleon Press, 1982)
125	Harper Baikie, *A Boy and His Axe* (private publisher, 1991)
128	CRM aural history tape A29-1
129	CRM aural history tape A216
130	W. Kaye Lamb, ed., *The Voyage of George Vancouver, 1791-1795* (London: Hakluyt Society, 1984)
131	Ezra Meeker, *Pioneer Reminiscences of Puget Sound* (Lowman & Hanford, 1905)
136	CRM aural history tape A48-1
137	*Musings*, Vol. IX, No. 2 (July 1990)
138	CRM MSS 88-22
139	*Campbell River Courier*, May 18, 1966, MSS 77-1
141	Francis Barrow log, CRM MSS 85-1
142	CRM aural history tape A184
144	Tom Henry, *Paul Bunyan on the West Coast* (Madeira Park BC: Harbour, 1995)
147	Harper Baikie, *A Boy and His Axe* (private publisher, 1991)
150	W. Kaye Lamb, ed., *The Voyage of George Vancouver, 1791-1795* (London: Hakluyt Society, 1984)
152	Journal of BC Exploratory Survey Trip into the Buttle's Lake Region by H. McC. Johnson, 1910, BCARS Add. MSS 249, Vol. 2, file 35
153	Excerpts from the diary of Andrew Muir 1848–1850, BCARS
158	CRM aural history tape, uncatalogued
159	CRM aural history tape, uncatalogued
162	Clellan S. Ford, *Smoke From Their Fires: The Life of a Kwakiutl Chief* (New Haven CT: Yale University Press, 1941)
165	CRM Archives, Marlatt Collection, 1904 letter
166	W. Kaye Lamb, ed., *The Voyage of George Vancouver, 1791-1795* (London: Hakluyt Society, 1984)
170	Excerpt from diary of Fred Nunns, BCARS; copy in CRM
179	Excerpt from diary of Fred Nunns, BCARS; copy in CRM
180–81	*Musings*, Vol. VII, No. 2
189	CRM aural history tape A233
194	*Musings,* Vol. IX, No. 3 (November 1990)
195	CRM MSS 87-68a, copy Katie Walker Clarke letter; original held by Joy Walker Huntley
197	Sir John Rogers, *Sport in Vancouver and Newfoundland* (London: Chapman & Hall Ltd., 1912)
198	CRM aural history tape A141
204	Left: CRM aural history tape A68-1; Right: CRM aural history tape A233
205	Jay Morrison, "The Magazine," December 1982 (newspaper clipping), CRM Archives, vertical file
206	CRM Archives, Gladys Knappett letter
211	CRM MSS 88-22
212	Harper Baikie, *A Boy and His Axe* (private publisher, 1991)
213	CRM MSS 88-22
214	CRM aural history tape A48-1